Sunset

An Illustrated Guide to

Organic Gardening

By the Editors of Sunset Books and Sunset Magazine

At Fetzer Vineyards a market gardener's delight: egg-plants, potatoes, beans, melons, cucumber, and herbs.

Sunset Publishing Corporation ■ Menlo Park, California

The lizard is one of several insect-eating allies (see page 52).

Research & Text
Bob Thompson

Coordinating Editor
Linda J. Selden

Design
Joe di Chiarro

Illustrations
Jane McCreary

Photographers: **Scott Camazine:** 59 top, 61 middle and bottom, 67 top, 68 top; **James L. Castner:** 5 top, 49 middle, 59 bottom, 60 top, 68 middle; **COMSTOCK/ Jack Clark:** 58 bottom, 64 top; **Rosalind Creasy:** 10, 11, 78; **Derek Fell:** 85; **Grant Heilman/Grant Heilman Photography Inc.:** 58 top, 61 top, 64 middle, 71 upper middle; **Saxon Holt:** 1, 5 bottom right, 6, 26, 72, 76, 94; **Charles Mann:** 8; **Ells Marugg:** 92; **Arthur H. McCain:** 71 bottom; **Jack McDowell:** 86; **Scott Millard:** 9; **Robert and Linda Mitchell:** 2, 49 top, 50 bottom left, 51 top, 57 top, 58 upper middle, 60 middle and bottom, 62 middle, 64 bottom, 65, 66; **Brad Nelson/ Nelson-Bohart & Associates:** 50 bottom right, 52, 63 middle; **Paul Peterson:** 50 middle left; **Norman A. Plate:** 82; **James H. Robinson:** 48, 49 bottom, 50 top and middle right, 51 upper middle, 63 top; **Bill Ross/West Light:** 88; **Runk/Schoenberger/ Grant Heilman Photography Inc.:** 46, 57 bottom, 58 lower middle, 59 middle, 62 top and bottom, 63 bottom, 67 bottom, 68 bottom, 69, 70, 71 top and lower middle; **John Shaw:** 51 lower middle and bottom; **Bill Stephens:** 91; **K. Bryan Swezey:** 43; **Darrow M. Watt:** 75, 81; **Tom Wyatt:** 5 left, 18, 24, 25, 29, 30, 31, 32, 33, 34, 35, 53, 54, 55, 56.

Back to the Future?

If you were a "back to the earth" baby of the 1960s, you may have cut your teeth on organically grown beets and groats. If you started out in life prior to 1946, the American soil and everything grown in it were innocent, as yet, of modern chemical fertilizers and pesticides.

As old a method as nature itself, organic gardening keeps making a come back because it makes good sense. During its revival in the sixties and seventies, when it was associated with vegetarian and ecological idealism, it became almost a religion for some. Helping to establish organic gardening as a mainstream topic, *Sunset Books* published the first edition of this title in 1971. Today, prompted by mounting statistics that show natural agricultural controls work better in the long haul than chemicals, cool-minded scientists advocate going organic. Accumulated evidence also warns that excessive use of chemical fertilizers and pesticides are unhealthy for both our digestive tracts and our land.

Many gardeners are now turning back their clocks and going organic, too. If you're one of them, you may have found that, like other old-fashioned ways of doing things, organic gardening takes more time and sweat than modern methods: it may involve new tools, techniques, and plant selections.

But the rewards will be great if you let this book guide you, gradually, to realistic success in a some-times frustrating field. Just take a clean bite out of one of your organic apples, and see if you'll ever go "modern" again.

For their expert help with preparing the text we wish to thank Dr. George E. Bohart; John R. Dunmire; Rusty Eddy; Forni-Brown Vegetables; Michael Maltas; Hugh Rackleff; Philip Sinclair; and the Cooperative Extension Services of University of Arizona, University of California, Colorado State University, Cornell University, University of Georgia, University of Missouri, Virginia Polytechnic Institute and State University, and Washington State University.

We also wish to thank JoAnn Masaoka Van Atta and Susan Bryant for assisting with photography and Pamela Evans for editing the manuscript.

Cover: Organically grown bounty with a southwestern slant includes chiles, tomatoes, tomatillos, pumpkins, sunflowers, blue corn, Mexican sage, and chayotes—and only begins to suggest the range and richness of the garden from which it comes. Cover design by Susan Bryant. Photography by Rosalind Creasy.

Editor, Sunset Books: Elizabeth L. Hogan

Third printing June 1991

CONTENTS

Special Features

THE ORGANIC GARDEN: DREAM OR REALITY?

Organic gardening is no mystery: it's what your parents (or grandparents, or great-grandparents) did before 1946, when chemists learned how to make fertilizers and pesticides from carbon and then from other elements and compounds.

Organic gardeners weed by hand, squash bugs underfoot, and fertilize with manures. They expend more time and sweat than gardeners who opt for chemical assistance and they see less satisfying body counts of pests. On the other hand, they spend less money and have fewer doubts about whether they've damaged ecosystems and whether their digestive systems will be able to handle the results.

Many advocates of organic gardening practice it as a way of living, some of them with a commitment very close to religious zeal. Its detractors see failure, whole or partial, in the inevitable odd wormy apple, leaf chewed to lacework, and new sprout gnawed off at the ground. A few scorn the very idea.

As usual, a wavering line runs somewhere between the extremes, and is a reasonable place from which to begin. Recent scientific and popular opinion has begun to favor less dependency on chemicals. The fact is, chlordane has come and gone and earwigs are still with us. The fact is, there *is* organically grown produce out there that looks fine and tastes great.

Increasingly, science supports the view that natural controls can work best in the long run. In Washington state, to give just one back-to-the-future example, for almost a century damage to orchard apples by three different species of mites was kept within tolerable limits by a natural predator, yet another species of mite. After the insecticide kelthane was introduced in the 1960s it nearly wiped out the predator species at the same time it controlled the pests. However, enough of the predators survived for a kelthane-resistant strain to emerge while enough of the pests survived for resistant strains of *them* to flourish. Now the new strain of predator mites is allowing growers to keep the new strains of the pests in check without kelthane. To bring the story full circle, kelthane recently has been banned from use.

Science seldom supports the most enthusiastic claims of amateur organic gardeners, however. Some will interplant potatoes and squash in a year when neither Colorado potato beetles nor squash bugs are plentiful, then claim to have found the perfect "companion" planting—one in which each plant drives off the other's pest with pheromones or some other scenting compound. Such claims almost always disappoint, making middle-of-the road expectations the safest ones to follow. The surest sources of information and inspiration are those who have to make an idea work.

In recent years upscale restaurants and specialty food stores across the continent have offered a steady market for commercial organic growers—often called market gardeners because they operate on a tiny scale compared to the majority of professional farmers. From their ranks come the most reasoned descriptions of how effective organic gardening practices can be. They must care for anywhere from one to a dozen acres of every sort of edible and ornamental plant. Their produce has to have at least some eye appeal for consumers. And they have to make a living.

It is that last factor that makes them such thoughtful students of their job and that thus ranked them right alongside Cooperative Agricultural Extension scientists as the most sought-after sources of information for this book.

They admit that not everything goes right all the time. On occasion, one of them reports, a whole planting has to be pulled out because some pest or disease has gotten so far ahead of the controls that the crop is unsaleable if not inedible. On rarer occasions, growers in a particular region have given up entirely on a particular kind of plant because it is so beset with problems as to be uneconomical.

The same market gardeners who have lost crops will hasten to say that they are not about to abandon organic techniques. The longer the garden goes on, they find, the less trouble they have with pests and diseases, because natural controls take over.

Successful organic gardening at home takes a similar long-term commitment to doing with muscles what might be done faster with chemicals, and the same long-term acceptance of occasional failures. Just how occasional the failures are may depend on how frequent are the muscular exertions.

As much as possible the information in this book sticks to facts that differentiate the organic way of gardening from the style that uses manufactured pesticides, herbicides, and fertilizers. These pages will tell you little or nothing about where or how to spread fertilizer, how to water, how to prune trees, or how to landscape your garden. (A couple of other *Sunset* books could come in handy—*Basic Gardening Illustrated*, *Pruning Handbook*, and *Landscaping Illustrated*.)

This book, we trust, will help get you off to a good start.

Organic approaches to master are building and maintaining balanced, healthy soil, knowing beneficial insects from pests, and choosing and protecting sturdy plants.

GETTING STARTED

Throw out the insecticides, throw out the manufactured fertilizers, and then what do you do? On a new site, perhaps everything. In a well-established, prosperous garden, perhaps not much—or then again perhaps quite a bit, especially if the focus is going to shift from low-maintenance ornamentals to high-density food crops. Whatever your starting point, there are five points to consider in planning your organic garden—devise an overall strategy, determine the orientation of the garden to the sun and wind, take stock of the soil, survey your tools and equipment, and decide on your plant selection.

Strategy is often overlooked until it's too late. Because successful organic gardening relies more on muscle and time than do other kinds, newcomers to the idea are well advised to take a long look at their personal calendars as well as at the seasons before they stock every available square foot with high-maintenance plants.

Assessing the basic facts of orientation allows you to match plants to their ideal conditions—to put shade-lovers in shade and sun-seekers in sun. Organic gardening adds another challenge: in all climates, but especially in damp ones, the sun and wind will have to take over some of the functions of chemicals to combat molds, mildews, and rots.

Healthy, productive soil is as vital an asset as intelligent plant placement, because it makes plants sturdier in the face of diseases and insects. Well-nourished soil means quick-starting, fast-growing seedlings that escape feeding insects while scrawny, stunted specimens remain prey. Healthy older plants endure damage with greater ease than struggling ones and are less likely to attract pests.

A beefed-up array of tools and equipment does the rest of the job of replacing herbicides, pesticides, and all the othercides in the day-to-day management of an organic garden. It is not only a matter of shovels and hoes, but also of traps, shields, and other mechanical devices that keep pests at bay. The tool shed is one of the last things a newcomer to the game thinks about, but is normally the first to be used.

Plant selection to eliminate or at least minimize known disease- or insect-prone species or varieties is a vast subject in itself, maybe the most important single aspect of all. A detailed discussion of how to make your choices begins on page 72.

One great advantage of organic gardening is that it's a race better suited to tortoises than hares, a job that need not be done overnight or even in a single growing season. In fact, heroic campaigns to improve the world of your garden in a day should be attempted only in the direst of circumstances. In all probability, the soil in your present garden will be in pretty good shape—improvable, no doubt, but no disaster. Just as probably, most of the healthy plants in that garden will be well suited to the exact spot in which they grow. When that is the case, trying to do too much too soon is apt to make things worse rather than better.

At Santa Fe, herbs dominate this organic garden: bee balm and common wormwood (left of wagon wheel), sage (in front of pedestal) and lemon verbena (in pot), lavender and lovage (behind statue).

SETTING A STRATEGY

The United States already boasts a large population of green-thumbers who stumbled into organic gardening full of hopes and ideals and stumbled back out within the year, blistered and cursing.

Some came to it so terrorized by the idea that the food they were buying in stores had been poisoned to some degree that they wanted to grow all of their own edibles starting right now. Others hoped to do something to help an earth they saw as battered into perilous straits by human industry. What they lacked in their bag of tools was a realistic strategy to make their dreams come true.

And so the first rule is this: Taking stock of a gar-den site should begin with assessing the gardener. Here are its corollaries:

1. Bite off a little bit less than you can chew, es-pecially if you are at the base of the learning curve with regard to gardening in general and organic gar-dening in particular. Trying too much too soon in-vites burnout.

One way to limit the load is to plant only half of your available area to things you want to grow for food or ornament while building more productive soil in the other half by sowing a leguminous cover crop, sheet composting, or using similar techniques. When the improved half is out of hospital, plant it with de-sired crops and begin reconditioning the soil of the first half. By the time both halves enjoy rich soil, your experience will make the doubled area easier to care for than either half was at the start.

In the Los Angeles County Arboretum's Henry Soto garden, organically grown, drought-tolerant plants include (front to back) lemon thyme, yellow gazanias, and salmon-hued Chasmanthe.

2. Begin by using the most, not the least, promising part of the property. It will be less frustrating. Save the more difficult parts of your site until experience has taught you a few lessons.

"Most promising" in this case can mean several things beyond the part with the most favorable exposure and most productive soil. For example, flat ground is easier to work than a slope. Being sited handy to water counts. Being in full view from your living room helps with motivation.

3. Before planting a large edible garden, sort out the family schedule. Edibles have a habit of ripening all at once, which means a flurry of preserving. They also have a knack of being ready to pick on the second or third day of your family's annual vacation.

4. Stick with plant species you like. They help keep you motivated if the going gets tough.

5. Don't insist on growing old favorites from other places. In our mobile society, many people who spent their working lives in Buffalo or Chicago retire to Tucson or Orlando, migrating with deep attachments to plants that are altogether ill suited to their new climate. (For old time's sake, grow one favorite in a pot that can be moved around to thwart damage by the new climate.)

6. Don't get attached to any individual plant too soon; not everything is going to work the first time. Keeping a little emotional distance lowers your frustration level.

7. Look to a broader horizon than your own property lines. What your neighbor grows, and how, will affect your own prospects. Extra defensive measures may be needed. Bugs are not dumb enough to stay in a war zone when asylum is right next door.

MAKING THE BEST OF THE SUN

Successful gardening depends, in very large part, on exactly how a plot stands in relation to the sun.

The orderly, mechanical approach to assessing this is to learn everything possible about regional temperature and rainfall patterns, plot the sun's track, and then fine-tune as required by the precise micro-climate of town, neighborhood, individual property, and internal details within your property.

From a slightly different perspective, it is a matter of studying what one veteran organic farmer has called the "polarities of air and earth, hot and cold, dry and wet."

Pure deserts are airy, hot, and dry. Temperate-zone rain forests are earthy, cool, and wet. From this per-

Near San Francisco, a lush private garden grows (front to back) nasturtiums, a salad of chard, tomatoes, and basil, sunflowers, globe amaranth, and, on the trellis, an Italian squash.

spective, your job in either place is to nudge the garden environment toward the central balance required by the sorts of plants you choose to grow. In a sandy desert the trick would be to create cooling shade and to improve soil texture to get full use out of every drop of water. In a cool, wet forest the task would be to get rid of some shade and moisture. Only a handful of people live at nature's extremes, but not many more live at a point of perfect or even near-perfect balance.

The majority of us get along by tinkering and adjusting soil and shade in one direction or the other. Those ultra-ambitious in their plant selection may have to go both ways at once.

On the following four pages are examples of when and how to modify these polarized growing conditions: cool-wet climates come first, hot-dry ones next. (Soils can be considered in the same light; notes on them begin on page 16.)

Near Seattle, an edible garden holds rich crops of (front to back) a mixed planting of tomatoes and borage, a row of assorted zucchinis, and kale.

Raise beds enough to keep roots above water table; use railroad ties or other treated wood.

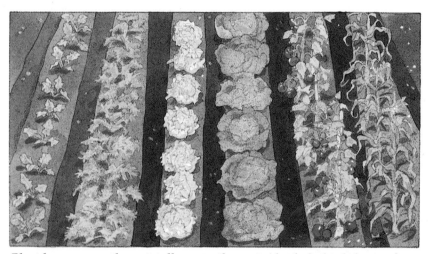

Plant low crops on the east, tall ones on the west side of a bed to help morning sun warm the soil.

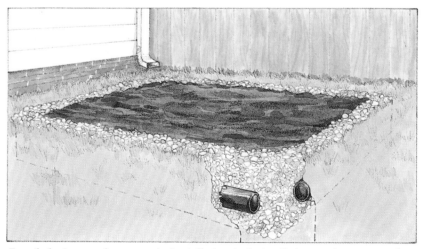

French drains cure boggy spots; install plastic drain tile in a perimeter gravel trough leading to a sump.

COOL-WET CLIMATE

Organic gardening in a cool, wet climate is a bit like driving on snow: all the normal rules apply, but the effects are exaggerated. The basic challenge is to maximize the sun and minimize the damp.

1. For vegetables, berries, and other edibles, set aside areas with excellent all-day exposure to light, especially morning sunlight. Warm soil early in the day helps plants grow and bear quickly. This is particularly important where growing seasons are short.

2. As far as possible, lay out several separate beds for edibles so that crops can be rotated annually.

3. Use south slopes or south-facing fences or screens to gain reflected warmth or to shelter heat-loving plants from cooling winds. Painting fences and screens in light colors helps reflect warmth.

4. Keep all food and ornamental planting beds well beyond the drip lines of trees; not only do trees cast unwanted shade, but their feeder roots swiftly invade fertile soils. The more heat the plants require, the more urgent full light is.

5. In the dampest, shadiest spots, try at least to achieve unhampered air flow; remove diseased and unwanted plants to open up constricted areas and improve conditions for healthier ones.

6. Defer the planting of eternally shady spots, especially where summer rains are frequent. Select only shade-loving plants resistant to rots, mildews, and molds. Natives are usually your best bet.

7. Avoid planting in boggy spots or, better, cure them with improved drainage (see at left).

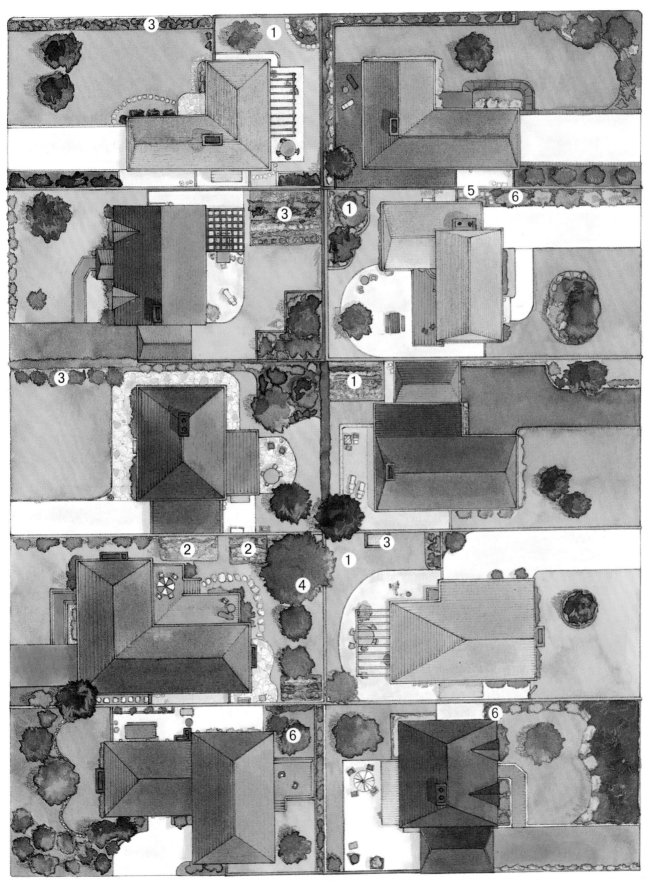

A quartet of trees can be used to shade a section of the garden, protecting sun-sensitive plants.

Drip irrigation is an easily installed means of economizing on water in desert or near-desert conditions.

A sunken bed of highly organic soil conserves water and will be more even in temperature than a raised bed.

HOT-DRY CLIMATE

To the degree that heat and dryness inhibit dozens of hard-to-control molds and rots, gardening organically in hot, dry climates is easier than in any damp one. In fact, expert gardeners in most humid regions say that rather than save seeds or cuttings from their own gardens they buy fresh materials from hot, dry regions every spring exactly for that reason.

On the down side, gardeners in hot, dry zones must work with a narrower range of plants, all of which are more likely to expire from one day to the next because of excessive heat or lack of moisture than they would in mild climates. Thus, the essential goal is to minimize heat and conserve moisture.

1. Install drip irrigation systems to supply all planting beds (see at left). Drip systems both conserve water and minimize the time spent watering.

2. Use structures to shade vegetables, berries, and other edibles from all-day sun, especially afternoon sun. Beds close to north walls will be coolest.

3. Sun-sensitive annual ornamentals may prosper directly under large shade trees if the soil is rich enough.

4. Sink planting beds below grade. This slows evaporation; with mulch, soil temperatures stay evener.

5. When sinking beds, maintain or even raise their borders to serve as windbreaks for seedlings (see at left).

6. If heat- and drought-resistant annual climbers such as beans are on your list, train them up a sunny wall of the house to ease the burden on your air-conditioning system. They die back in winter, allowing the sun to warm your house.

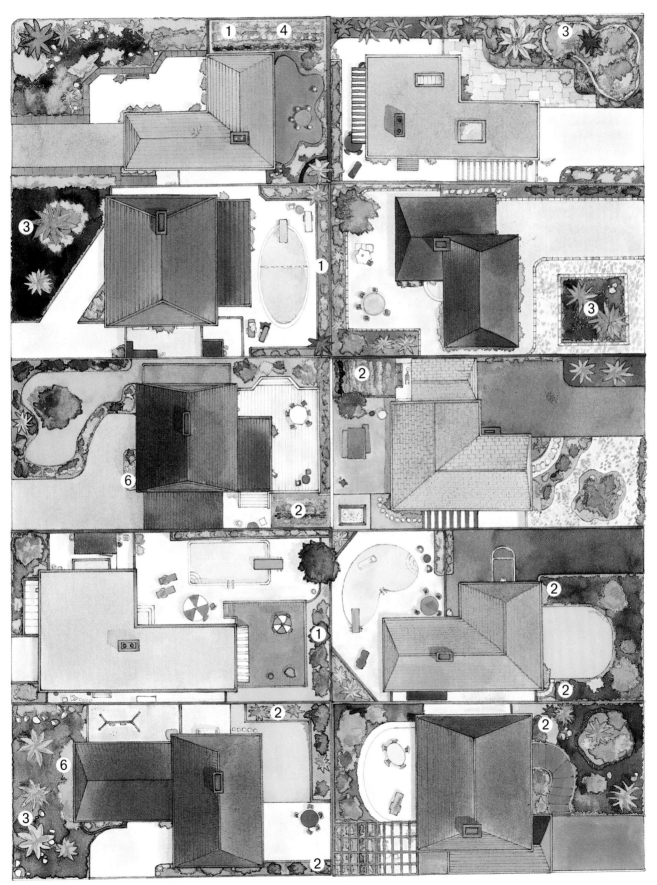

TAKING STOCK OF THE SOIL

Any patch of soil that will grow a healthy crop of weeds will also grow desirable plants. But any organic gardener hopeful of success will do well to push the soil quality from passable toward optimal.

Understanding soil in all its complexity is a life's work. For a gardener, the simple questions are these:

- How deep does it go?
- How well does it drain?
- How rich is it in nutrients?
- Is it acidic or alkaline?

Soil from Top to Bottom

Simple definitions of the layers in an undisturbed soil are as follows, from top to bottom:

Surface. The top fraction, l to 2 inches deep, is made up of a miscellany of undecomposed and decomposed organic matter.

Topsoil. The next several inches (to a typical maximum of 10) are mostly mineral but may be enriched with as much as 20 percent organic matter. This is the layer organic gardeners must work to enrich and deepen.

Edible and ornamental annuals fare best when the topsoil is at least as deep as their root zones. The art shows the optimal root depth of several favorites.

Subsoil. Nutrients and clays leached from the topsoil accumulate in this band, which may reach to a depth of 30 inches. The band may contain nutrient-bearing clay and humus in some combination. Its structure is still developing. Subsoil tends to be more compacted than surface soil, especially after the latter has been tilled for some time. If it's too compacted, it inhibits root development and water penetration.

Sometimes subsoil is divided into two sublayers: an upper one, from which most of the nutrients have been leached, and a lower one, in which those same nutrients have accumulated.

Parent soil. Any unsolidified material below the layers of active soil formation is the parent soil. It is significant primarily in providing minerals to the layers above.

Bedrock. Typically bedrock begins about 48 inches below the surface, except where grading or erosion has disturbed soil development.

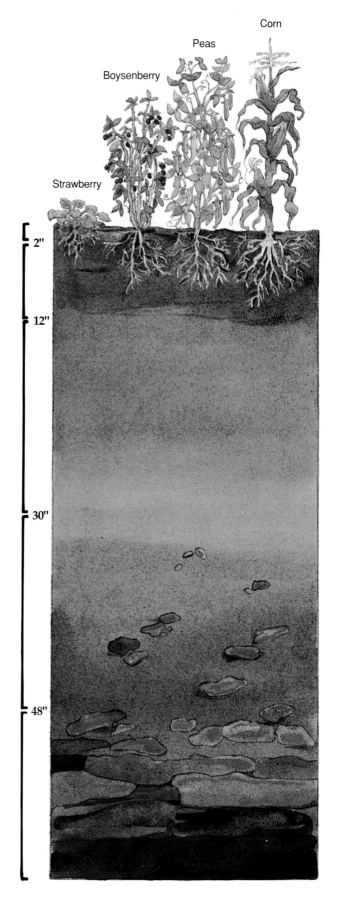

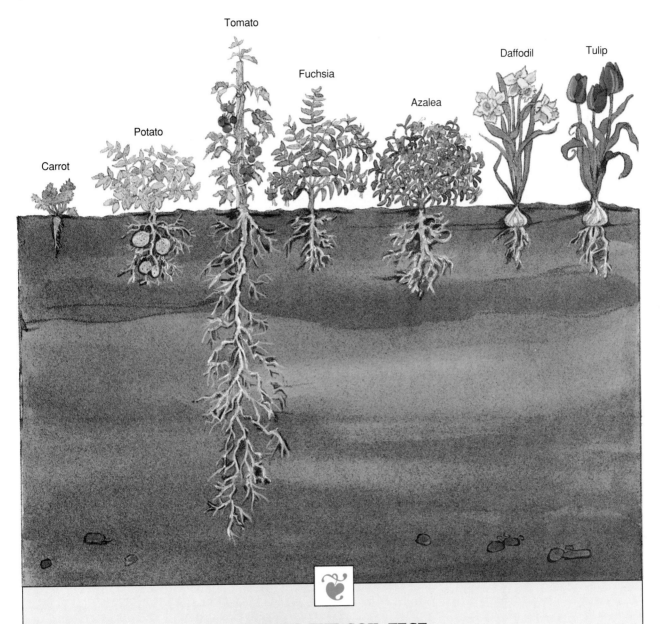

Carrot Potato Tomato Fuchsia Azalea Daffodil Tulip

TAKING THE SOIL TEST

In a new garden, a soil test can save time and effort in establishing productive soil. Home test kits will reveal the pH (the balance between acid and alkali; see page 19). Professional laboratory tests in addition measure phosphorus (P) and potassium (K); see page 21. Trace minerals can also be measured if there is reason to suspect an imbalance. Testing need be done only once provided you follow up on it by building well-balanced soil.

The key is to take a proper sample. Experts recommend the following: With a shovel or soil probe, take six to a dozen samples randomly throughout the garden. Observe any changes in appearance of the soil within the garden, taking samples from each soil type if you have more than one. Each sample should be at least 4 inches deep; 6 is better. Mix each sample, pulverizing any clods, so the soil is completely homogenized. Then mix all the samples together thoroughly. Seal a 1-pint sample to send to a lab. For a home test, allow the sample to air-dry first.

Some Agricultural Extension agents also perform soil tests; those who do not can recommend a professional lab. Extension agent telephone numbers are in the government listings of the white pages.

Pure clay (dry at left, saturated at right)

Pure sand (dry at left, saturated at right)

Pure humus (dry at left, saturated at right)

Clay loam (dry at left, saturated at right)

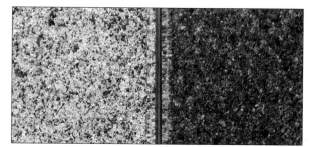

Sandy loam (dry at left, saturated at right)

CLASSIFYING YOUR SOIL

As far as mineral soils go, the textural opposites are fine clay and coarse sand. Each type offers both benefits and drawbacks to the gardener. Correcting soil with organic matter removes the drawbacks and leaves the virtues in both, resulting in rich soils called "loams."

Clay. Even the largest particles in clay are microscopic; about 100 would fit into the period that ends this sentence. Clay is slow to both warm and cool. It absorbs moisture slowly, retaining it for long periods. When wet it excludes oxygen, inhibiting root development among other things. Working it wet means it will dry as hard as a clay pot. Working it dry further pulverizes it. Clay soils therefore should be tilled only when barely moist enough to crumble in the hand. To offset its drawbacks, clay can be rich in nutrients and is slow to lose added nutrients by leaching.

Sand. The smallest particles of sand are more than 25 times larger than the largest particles of clay. Sand warms and cools quickly. Water drains through it swiftly, carrying nutrients into the subsoil below. Sand can be tilled easily at any time and admits oxygen for roots. It's good for some root crops because it displaces so easily, but it typically loses nutrients through leaching, so plants in it require frequent feeding.

Humus. As completely or nearly completely decomposed organic matter, humus helps create a very rich, moisture-retaining soil. Its richness and texture discourage some pests and diseases, but humus may also lack one or more minerals required by plants. It helps sandy soils retain moisture and nutrients and helps open clayey soils to air and water penetration.

Clay loam. Clayey soils loosened with organic matter are still heavy but are tillable, with high nutrient value and excellent moisture-holding properties. They are most useful in hot, dry climates.

Sandy loam. Sandy soils made less porous with organic matter remain easily tillable but are better able than pure sand to retain both nutrients and moisture. They still may require frequent fertilization. Sandy loams are most useful in cool, damp climates.

ACIDIC OR ALKALINE?... WHAT pH MEANS

The pH of elements is one of the minor mysteries of American daily life; it comes up when conversation turns to wine, swimming pool water, milk products, or garden soil. It is short for *potential Hydrogen*, and is a measure of the activity of acid in a material.

Neutral measures 7.0 on the pH scale. Less than 7 is acidic; more is alkaline.

Most plants thrive in soils with pH levels of 6.0 to 6.8. Blueberries, which are among the most acid-tolerant plants, will perform at pH levels as low as 4.5. Many desert plants (and especially Australian ones) will grow well in soils having a pH of up to 8.0.

The lists below may help you diagnose the pH of the soil in an established garden: observe which of these plants are thriving and which are struggling. (Do not use them as your only guide; other factors may lead to poor performance.) The lists also may be used to group plants with similar soil requirements; again, keep in mind that drainage and other factors must be considered.

Most plants cannot extract nutrients from unbalanced soils. At a pH of 8.0, potassium, nitrates, phosphates, iron, and manganese become unavailable. At a pH of below 4.5 plants cannot take up nitrates, magnesium, or phosphates. Also, some elements become overly available and thus toxic.

For specific correctives, see page 28. For how to test soil, see page 17.

PLANT TOLERANCE OF SOIL pH

Alkaline tolerant (pH of 7.0 to 8.0)	Slightly acid tolerant (pH of 6.0 to 6.8)	Moderately acid tolerant (pH of 5.5 to 6.8)	Very acid tolerant (pH of 5.0 to 6.8)
acacia	asparagus	bean	azalea
bottlebrush	beet	begonia	blueberry
date palms	bok choy	Brussels sprouts	chicory
dusty miller	broccoli	calla	endive
eucalyptus	cabbage	camellia	heathers
geranium	cauliflower	carrot	hydrangea
oleander	chard	collard greens	Irish potato
olive	lettuce	corn	rhododendron
periwinkle	muskmelon	cucumber	rhubarb
pink	okra	eggplant	shallot
pomegranate	onion	fuchsia	sorrel
salt cedar	peanut	garlic	sweet potato
tamarisk	spinach	kale	watermelon
thyme		kohlrabi	
		Lima bean	
		parsley	
		pea	
		peppers	
		pumpkin	
		radish	
		rutabaga	
		soybean	
		squash	
		sunflower	
		tomato	
		turnip	
		viola	

SYMPTOMS OF NUTRIENT DEFICIENCY

Symptom	Deficiency				
	Nitrogen	Phosphorus	Potassium	Iron	Magnesium
Sickly, yellow-green leaf color	■			■	
Slow growth, dwarfing	■	■			
Drying of lower leaves	■		■		
Purplish leaves, stems, and branches		■			
Poor flower production		■			
Mottling, spotting, streaking, or curling, starting on lower leaves			■		
Complete loss of green on lower leaves; green veins in yellowed leaves higher on plant	■			■	■
Very pale yellow leaves; veins remain green until leaf is nearly white; shows earliest at tips of branches				■	■

TRACE ELEMENT DEFICIENCIES

All of the following deficiencies are rare in soil with a proper organic component; they are usually cured by organic amendments if they do exist.

Some trace elements may be present but unavailable to plants if the pH of the soil is severely unbalanced (see page 19). A severe calcium deficiency may require the addition of some lime.

Boron. The first symptom is corky fruit. More severe deficiencies are revealed by dying tip growth, withered blossoms, deformed leaves, and failure of flowers to form. It is easiest to see in early spring.

Calcium. Young leaves yellow, then brown; tip growth curls; stems weaken; roots are shorter than normal.

Copper. Sometimes called "wither tip," the deficiency is marked by tip leaves yellowing, withering, and falling in mid-June after a normal beginning. Leaves sometimes look overly long before they fall.

Manganese. Areas between veins of older leaves lighten, as with iron chlorosis; dead spots on the leaves are even surer signs. Over time the plant becomes stunted.

Molybdenum. Plant is very stunted, with pallid, distorted leaves.

Sulfur. Stems are hard, brittle, and thinner than normal. Lower leaves turn yellow.

Zinc. Tip leaves are small; distance between leaves may lessen greatly. Some leaves may have dead areas. Buds do not form.

N, P, K—AND THE SUPPORTING CAST

The building blocks of healthy plant growth are nitrogen (N), phosphorus (P), and potassium (K); these are supplemented by the important elements iron and magnesium, and seven trace elements (boron, calcium, copper, manganese, molybdenum, sulfur, and zinc).

Nitrogen in the soil governs a plant's capacity to manufacture proteins, the growth promoters in each cell. Leaf growth, especially, requires large volumes of nitrogen, so it must be replenished in the soil. Being soluble, it is also lost by leaching, especially in sandy soils in wet climates. Yellowing older leaves distant from growth tips are the principal symptom of nitrogen deficiency. Blood meal and hoof-and-horn meal are high-nitrogen organic fertilizers, but many others will serve the purpose.

Phosphorus is necessary to the production of plant sugars and is the mechanism by which sugars move within a plant. Symptoms of phosphorus deficiency are similar to those of nitrogen deficiency, except that leaves may be duller green than normal or have a purplish tint. Extremely acidic soils are most likely to be phosphorus deficient. Bonemeal and wood ashes contain this mineral.

Potassium is also crucial to the manufacture and movement of sugar and starches within a plant; it seems especially important to seed production. A deficiency is revealed in yellow or burnt-looking leaf margins. Because plants take potassium up from soil, it must be replenished there. Granite dust and hardwood ashes are useful sources.

Except in soils of extremely low organic content, the other minerals and elements are rarely deficient; organic soil conditioners will add or maintain adequate amounts.

NITROGEN REQUIREMENTS OF EDIBLE PLANTS

Light feeders	Medium feeders	Heavy feeders
apple	asparagus	artichoke
beans (with inoculant)	beans (all)	avocado
fava bean	beet	broccoli
grape	carrot	cabbage
Jerusalem artichoke	chard	cauliflower
pea	cucumber	celery
peach	eggplant	citrus fruits
pear	greens (except lettuce)	corn
plum	herbs	Irish potato
salsify	melons (all)	lettuce
southern pea	okra	onion
strawberry	peanut	pumpkin
	peppers	sweet potato
	radish	tomato
	rhubarb	
	spinach	
	squash	
	sunflower	
	turnip	

STAYING A STEP AHEAD OF TROUBLE

Rotating edible crops annually helps keep soils fertile and inhibits the proliferation of pests and disease organisms.

As the lists on page 21 show, some plants are heavy feeders, depleting the soil's nutrients rapidly, but others feed lightly. Tomatoes and potatoes are notoriously prone to soilborne diseases that prosper if these hosts go into the same ground year after year. Members of any group of closely related plants should not succeed each other for several years in a row, because relatives will likely prove subject to the same pests and diseases. The coles—cabbage, cauliflower, radishes, turnips, and so on—are an easy-to-remember example, but tomatoes and their family are a more important one because they are much more disease prone.

Experts recommend a 4- to 6-year rotation scheme for home gardens. But the same experts say the best systems are intuitive, born of experience. Great, but everybody has to start somewhere. The first plan shown below is based on the dominant parts of plants; the second, on the facing page, is slightly more specific. Both are simplified in the extreme. Adding other vegetables, small fruits, or ornamentals to one or more beds would not change the basic plan, as long as they were similar feeders that didn't introduce pests or diseases to the principal planting.

Year 1

Year 3

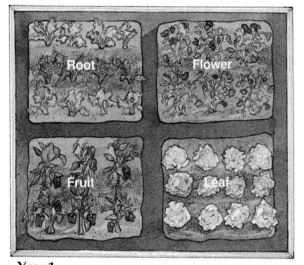

Year 2

Year 4

FAMILIES OF EDIBLE PLANTS

To avoid buildup of pests and disease organisms, the following related plants should be grown together and moved together—or at least should not succeed each other in the same soil.

■ (most susceptible) eggplant, peppers, potatoes, tomatoes ■ chives, garlic, leeks, onions, shallots ■ beets, spinach, Swiss chard ■ bok choy, broccoli, Brussels sprouts, cabbage, cauliflower, collards, kale, kohlrabi, mustard, rutabagas, turnips ■ broad beans, Lima beans, peas, snap beans ■ carrots, celeriac, celery, parsley, parsnips ■ cucumbers, muskmelons, pumpkins, squash, watermelons ■ endive, lettuce, salsify

Year 3

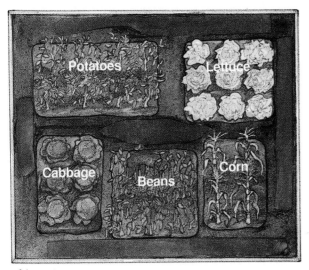

Year 1

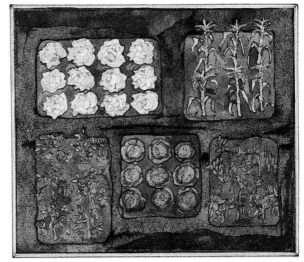

Year 4

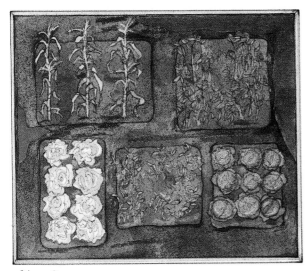

Year 2

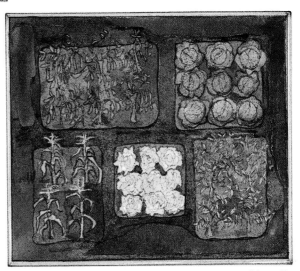

Year 5

An organic gardener's equipment must include several defenses against pests. A good quality sprayer for organic pesticides and a sticky barrier do away with pests. Cages and nets of various sizes hold them at bay. (Recycle milk cartons and berry baskets rather than buying manufactured cages.) Pheromone traps (at top) are mostly to help identify pests.

THE TOOL SHED

As in other kinds of gardening, the essential tools for cultivation are one shovel or spade, one rake, and one hoe. The shovel turns the soil, the rake pulverizes and levels it, and the hoe slices off weeds. Owning a broader selection of each will save muscle power, because the many variations in shape and size are tailored to specific tasks. Pruning tools are no different for organic gardens than for chemically managed ones.

Purists, incidentally, look askance at the organic gardener who brings power tools to a plot of 1,000 square feet or less. Some of them get quite sharp over the idea of a rotary tiller replacing a spade, for instance, feeling that it does not till deep enough and that it compacts the soil 6 to 9 inches below the surface.

The organic gardener's equipment differs most from a chemical-oriented practitioner's in the addition of traps, baffles, and other devices meant to keep pests at bay.

Essential garden tools should include (left to right) a bow rake for leveling soil and pulverizing clods; a metal or bamboo lawn rake for collecting fallen leaves and other debris; a spade for turning soil in preparation for planting or for moving soil; and a turning fork to loosen soil, harvest root crops, turn compost. Some would add a round-nosed shovel to turn soil.

Weed-control tools are (left to right) a cultivator hoe for uprooting weeds and forming planting trenches; a heavy weed cutter; a grass cutter; a standard garden hoe for cutting off weeds just below soil level; and two variations of the hula hoe, also for cutting off weeds just below soil level. Standard hoes cut on the pull stroke, hulas on the push.

BUILDING & MAINTAINING SOIL

It cannot be said too often: organic gardening is a process, almost a loop. Weed control, pest and disease control, and plant selection all play important, interconnected roles. However, healthy, biologically active soil makes the rest go round. One recipe for picture-perfect topsoil in a moderate climate with a long growing season is 25 percent moisture, 25 percent air, 45 percent mineral soil, and 5 percent organic matter. That is, the mineral soil is coarse textured enough to leave open half of any given volume of topsoil as channels for moisture and air, and the organic portion is just rich enough to keep nutrients and moisture available to plant roots. This basic recipe can be modified to suit other, more extreme climates. In deserts a heavier, more clayey soil would be better to help retain precious moisture. Such a soil is also slow to lose its nutrients, so it might be fertile enough with a more modest percentage of organic content. In a cool, wet climate a more open, sandy soil would help excess moisture drain away. But as sandy soils also allow nutrients to leach away swiftly, a higher proportion of organic material would almost always be in order. The formula is not a bad starting point, then, but it needs refinement. Some plants devour nitrogen rapaciously; others use little. Some demand more potassium or phosphorus than others. And so what is planted—or is about to be planted—matters almost as much as climate in building an ideal soil. Dense planting for high yield also changes the picture. Question Number One is this: what, if anything, needs to be changed to make your garden plan work? Pages 16–18 define soil types and show you ways to measure soil balance and nutrients to find out. Only if things are out of kilter does Question Number Two arise: how do you get from not-so-good to better? (For gardens, too, a basic rule is "If it ain't broke, don't fix it!") Task One is nutrition, and nutrition basically means maintaining nitrogen. Nitrogen replacement is an ongoing job for any soil. Tests or your own observation will turn up any other needs. Task Two is improving soil structure in order to make the moisture and nutrients you provide more effective. This, too, is a long-term project. Because the words organic and compost go together even more often than hand and glove, it should come as no surprise that compost is the organic gardener's first answer to most, sometimes all, shortcomings of an existing soil. As the nearest thing to an ideal combination of soil amendment and fertilizer all in one, its reputation is well earned. However, where a soil is far from healthy and productive, other materials can play important roles in speeding up the development of adequate soil. This chapter defines the major organic fertilizers and soil amendments and then shows how to put them to use.

FERTILIZERS & SOIL AMENDMENTS

Fertilizers and soil amendments are not the same thing. Fertilizers provide nutrients for plants. Amendments improve a soil's ability to keep nutrients and water available to plant roots—and they make soil easier to till.

But many organic materials fill both bills, so information on fertilizers and amendments is combined in this section, in alphabetic order. To simplify your search through the possibilities, an easy-reference list follows.

This is not an invitation to skip reading all the detailed entries. Some materials will do more than you want them to, creating a problem different from the one you sought to cure. For example, adding steer manure is a handy way to loosen heavy clay soils, but it contains salts and weed seeds, so it may not be as useful a solution as peat moss. Or say you have an acidic soil that needs to be "sweetened" with an alkaline additive. Limestone contains no potash; wood ashes are rich in it. If your soil has ample potash, either material might serve equally well. If, on the other hand, potash is lacking, wood ashes would cure both deficiencies for the price of one. Still other possibilities might push you to choose one or the other of these materials. For example, dolomitic limestone contains magnesium. That trace element is lacking in many soils in western Washington; however, it is abundant in other places—and excessive magnesium is toxic to some plants.

Some things that seem simple and sound logical are bad ideas. Mixing in sand sounds like a perfect way to loosen up clay. Wrong. It makes cement.

Whatever you choose to do, the first and most frequent advice from experienced organic gardeners is to go slow in amending soil. Plan on spending 3, 4, even 5 years getting the texture you want. Build a couple of raised beds and fill them with first-class soil if you want some quick results.

The temptation to hurry along is almost impossible to resist, especially when the garden is iron-hard clay, or all the plants out there—even the weeds—are stunted and struggling. However, trying to go too fast usually results in a different imbalance from the one you are trying to cure. For one thing, the pH can go up and down in bewildering ways as old soil and an amendment interact with one another.

One workable rule of thumb is to dig no more than 4 inches of organic material into the top 8 to 12 inches of soil per year. The more fully composted that material is, the better. The more evenly mixed soil and amendment are, the better.

Good mixing means thorough digging. The French intensive technique of double-digging (see page 44) is a useful strategy for getting new and old material to mix well in any garden, not just intensively cultivated ones.

While you are developing the structure of your soil, use all the other tricks in the bag:

- Choose annuals adapted to the existing soil (sometimes variety is as important as species).

- Tailor your watering to the soil type as carefully as possible—infrequent but deep soaks for clay, frequent but not lengthy soaks for sand.

- Use a mulch with some fertilizer value to help foundation plants get along at least passably well.

The detailed entries on soil amendments and fertilizers that follow are far from an exhaustive list. In fact they include only commonly available materials. Remember that the world is full of other organic by-products, of which seaweed, shellfish waste, nut hulls, comfrey leaves, cocoa bean hulls, and mushroom compost are only a few. Poking around among local industries may uncover these or still other low-cost materials of great benefit to your garden.

Each entry includes a note on fertilizer value that indicates N-P-K and a parenthetical notation of the speed of nitrogen release. Speed of release can be important. Fast fertilizers work best with food plants that ripen their crops quickly, such as strawberries; slow ones work best with crops that ripen slowly—root vegetables, for example.

Now, here are the quick summaries of which fertilizers and amendments to use for which situations:

To acidify: iron sulfate, sulfur

To alkalize: limestone (dolomitic or calcitic), oyster shell, wood ashes

For nitrogen: blood meal, bonemeal, chicken manure, cottonseed meal, fish meal

For phosphorus: bonemeal, chicken manure, fish meal, wood ashes

For potassium: kelp, wood ashes

To loosen clays: compost, manures, peat, sawdust

To enrich sands: compost, manures, peat, wood ashes

Mulches: compost, tree bark (ground), sawdust

BAT GUANO

Bat guano has been popular with gardeners in several different eras. In short supply now, it is one of the most expensive of fertilizers. Its fertilizer value varies with the source and processing technique.

Fertilizer value: 13–0–0, 10–4–1 (fast) or 1–6–0.5 (slow), depending on source

pH: slightly alkaline

Soil amendment value: none

Uses: as a quick-acting stimulant to early growth

Limitations: price almost limits it to container plants indoors or out

Sources: nurseries, mail order

BLOOD MEAL

As its name suggests, blood meal is a by-product of meat-packing plants.

Fertilizer value: 12–1.5–0.6 (medium)

pH: slightly acidic

Soil amendment value: none

Uses: as a quick-acting nitrogen fertilizer where no bulk is needed or wanted; often used as a side-dressing

Limitations: excess will burn foliage

Sources: nurseries and garden supply stores

BONEMEAL

Another by-product of meat-packing plants, bonemeal comes in two forms: raw and steamed. Though the raw form is a more powerful source of nitrogen, it's less recommended.

Fertilizer value: raw, 2 to 6–15 to 27–0 (slow); steamed, 0.7 to 4–18 to 34–0 (slow to medium)

pH: alkaline

Soil amendment value: none

Uses: especially useful where phosphorus is lacking

Limitations: none known

Sources: nurseries and garden supply stores; supplies very limited in some regions

CHICKEN MANURE

Poultry manure (chicken manure, in particular) offers one of the fastest, strongest nitrogen fixes available to organic gardeners. It is marketed with different moisture levels.

Fertilizer value: 15% moisture, 6–4–3 (medium to rapid); 30% moisture, 3–2.5–1.5 (medium to rapid); 75% moisture, 1.5–1–0.5 (medium to rapid)

pH: variable, generally alkaline

Soil amendment value: retains moisture well, so good in sandy soils

Uses: excellent for nitrogen-hungry leafy vegetables

Limitations: must be watered in well to prevent nitrogen burn, especially if used as a side-dressing; malodorous, especially when wet; some salts, though fewer than in steer manure

Sources: poultry farms, some garden supply stores

COMPOST

Compost is, purely and simply, plant material become earth again through bacterial action. The better the garden grows, the richer and larger the supply of raw material it gives back to itself.

Fertilizer value: 1.5 to 3.5–0.5 to 1–1 to 2 (slow)

pH: variable, but usually slightly acidic

Soil amendment value: good moisture retention; excellent nutrient holder; moderate in salts

Uses: as a gentle, slow-acting fertilizer; diminishes moisture content of clay and increases it in sand; keeps nutrients available to roots in sand

Limitations: possible pesticide residues can make resulting compost unfit for vegetable gardens

Sources: own garden, community composting projects, and—increasingly—nurseries

COTTONSEED MEAL

The ground-up seeds of cotton provide one of the more nutrient-rich combination fertilizers and soil conditioners available to organic gardeners.

Fertilizer value: 6–2.5–1.7 (slow to medium)

pH: acidic

Soil amendment value: good moisture retention; slow to decompose

Uses: good on slow-maturing root crops and sweet potatoes

Limitations: seedlings and small new plants can be burned when meal is applied directly in pure form

Sources: nurseries

DAIRY MANURE

Because dairy cattle are pen fed, their manure is preferable to steer manure, having lower salt and weed seed content. (*See also* chicken manure, steer manure.)

Fertilizer value: .25–.15–.25 (medium)

pH: variable, depending on animals' feed and bedding; generally alkaline

Soil amendment value: improves soil texture without risk of overfertilization

Uses: adds organic content to soils

Limitations: some salts are present

Sources: dairies, primarily

FISH MEAL

Some processors grind and cook the inedible parts of commercially caught fish into meal.

Fertilizer value: 10–4–0 (slow)

pH: acidic

Soil amendment value: none

Uses: as a slow-acting source of nitrogen; especially useful with sweet potatoes and root crops

Limitations: none known

Sources: nurseries

GRAPE POMACE

Wine making leaves behind the skins and seeds of grapes. The skins are pressed nearly dry in processing, forming a loosely caked mass called "pomace."

Fertilizer value: 3–0–0 (slow)

pH: acidic to very acidic

Soil amendment value: slow to decompose; excellent nutrient and moisture retention; salt-free

Uses: loosens clay; adds acidity to alkaline soils

Limitations: white wine (but not red wine) pomace sprouts grape seedlings profusely; at its freshest, smelly and attractive to fruit flies; best applied no earlier than the spring following harvest

Sources: primarily wineries; some wine country garden supply stores

HOOF-AND-HORN MEAL

Yet another by-product of the meat-processing industry, hoof-and-horn meal is used as is blood meal.

Fertilizer value: 12–2–0 (medium to slow)

pH: alkaline

Soil amendment value: none

Uses: as an excellent slow-release, nonburning side-dressing; can be mixed with sawdust or other nitrogen-binding soil amendments

Limitations: none known

Sources: nurseries

LIME

At its softest limestone is chalk, at its hardest, marble. In either form it is pure or nearly pure calcium carbonate, the great de-acidifier of soil.

Fertilizer value: none

pH: strongly alkaline

Soil amendment value: as a fine dust, may make soil heavier; ground coarser, will not, but works less quickly—perhaps not at all—at its primary job (See "How to Correct pH in Soil," page 38.)

Uses: de-acidifies unbalanced soil

Limitations: for soil low in phosphorus and potassium, wood ashes more suitable; measurable amounts of magnesium in dolomite or dolomitic (but not calcitic) limestone, so used principally where that mineral is lacking

Sources: nurseries, farm supply stores

(OAK) LEAF MOLD

As its name implies, leaf mold is a sort of one-note samba, a not fully decomposed compost of tree leaves.

Fertilizer value: 0.8–0.35–0.15 (slow)

pH: slightly acidic

Soil amendment value: excellent moisture and nutrient retention; fairly rapid decomposition

Uses: as an efficient mulch that can be dug in after the growing season to improve organic content

Limitations: may bind nitrogen (if symptoms appear, supplement nitrogen with side-dressing of, for example, blood meal or chicken manure)

Sources: some nurseries

OYSTER SHELLS

The shells of all bivalves contain high proportions of calcium carbonate, the most useful means of lowering acid levels in soil. However, only oysters are farmed intensively enough for their shells to be processed for garden use.

Fertilizer value: none

pH: strongly alkaline

Soil amendment value: typical coarse-ground texture speeds drainage

Uses: de-acidifies soils; will loosen clays

Limitations: a modest salt content if not well washed

Sources: specialist suppliers, mainly near commercial oyster beds; poultry and feed stores

PEAT

Peat is the residue of partially decomposed bog vegetation, most often mosses. The names of peats for gardening sometimes reflect the particular species or variety: hypnum, spaghnum, sedge.

Fertilizer value: 1.5 to 3–.25 to .5–.5 to 1 (very slow)

pH: acidic

Soil amendment value: coarse fibers loosen clays but also retain moisture; moisture-holding ability useful in sandy soils

Uses: as a soil amendment

Limitations: water repellent when dry, so should be dug into soil; too light to serve as a mulch

Sources: garden supply stores

RICE HULLS

Nearly weightless yet remarkably tough, rice hulls are left behind after grains of rice have been processed as food.

Fertilizer value: virtually none (but a trace of nitrogen)

pH: neutral

Soil amendment value: lightens soil; is slow to decompose

Uses: as a quick means of lightening heavy clay soils; in artificial soils for container gardening

Limitations: inefficient in holding nutrients or moisture, so normally used in combination with other organic materials

Sources: primarily rice processers; some feed stores (note: packaged in huge bags)

SAWDUSTS

This familiar by-product of lumber milling is not all alike. Various species of trees yield sawdust with different characteristics.

Fertilizer value: 4–2–4 (very slow)

pH: acidic

Soil amendment value: loosens heavy soils

Uses: as mulch, then slowly worked in as soil conditioner for slow-acting source of nitrogen

Limitations: tendency to bind nitrogen in raw form (especially redwood, pine, fir, and other conifer sawdust; alder and most hardwoods less problematic)—should be well aged or mixed with 12 pounds of chicken manure per 50 pounds of sawdust; inefficient retainer of nutrients; alder reputed especially prone to the fungus *Armillaria*

Sources: sawmills in logging country; some nurseries and garden supply stores

SEWAGE SLUDGE

Sewage sludge is exactly what you think, but treatment renders it an unobjectionable material to handle in a garden. Of its two main forms, activated (dried and heat treated) is preferred.

Fertilizer value: activated, 5 to 6–3 to 7–.8 (slow)

Soil amendment value: loosens heavy soils; improves moisture- and nutrient-holding capacities of sand

pH: slightly to strongly acidic

Uses: as a good soil conditioner; activated sludge (pH 4.5 to 5.5) as an acidifier

Limitations: can't be used on food plants because of possible cadmium or other heavy metals content—get analysis from sewer district; may burn seedlings or small bedding plants if not composted before use

Sources: increasingly, garden supply stores; municipalities, through local sewage treatment plants

STEER MANURE

Steer manure is one of the old standbys among soil conditioners—but not one of the most beloved, because the waste of beef animals contains unwanted salts and weed seeds. (*See also* dairy manure—and be aware that auction yards, fairgrounds, racetracks, circuses, and zoos can be occasional suppliers of other, sometimes better manures. Elephant dung has the best reputation as a fertilizer.)

Fertilizer value: .25–.15–.25 (medium)

pH: variable, depending on animals' feed and bedding; generally alkaline

Soil amendment value: improves moisture and nutrient retention in sand; loosens heavy soils

Uses: as an amendment to sandy soils

Limitations: can be high in salts, full of weed seeds

Sources: nurseries (in bags); feed lots (raw)

SULFUR

An elemental material, sulfur is best known as a fungicide and mildicide. However, in the coarse-ground form called "soil sulfur" it is the most effective acidifier of soil.

Fertilizer value: none

pH: highly acidic

Soil amendment value: none

Uses: corrects alkaline soils, especially for rhododendrons, azaleas, and other acid-loving plants; as a possible inhibitor of molds, fungi

Limitations: can burn foliage if applied during temperatures of more than 90°F

Sources: nurseries, farm supply stores

TREE BARK

The bark of various trees is often used as a mulch and sometimes as a soil conditioner. Most bark is sold as chips, but conifer bark, in particular, can be ground fine. Ground bark is increasingly popular, owing in part to its relative visual appeal.

Fertilizer value: 4–2–4 (slow)

pH: slightly acidic

Soil amendment value: improves moisture and nutrient retention in sandy soils (ground bark only)

Uses: as a good mulch; ground barks as soil conditioners and a slow-release nitrogen source if spaded in after being used as mulch

Limitations: raw bark—especially from conifers—tends to bind nitrogen unless treated

Sources: garden supply stores

WOOD ASHES

Fireplace or wood stove ashes contain 15 to 32 percent calcium carbonate, making them pound for pound almost exactly as alkaline as limestones. Hardwood ashes are more alkaline than softwood ashes and are also richer fertilizers.

Fertilizer value: 0–5 to 7–2 to 3 (fast)

pH: strongly alkaline

Soil amendment value: best suited to sandy soils; fine ashes can make clay soils even heavier

Uses: corrects overacidic soils; especially valuable where phosphorus or potassium are lacking

Limitations: problematic around plants requiring highly acidic soils; damaging to germinating seeds and new seedlings, which can be harmed by alkalinity—avoid by digging ashes into soil in late fall

Sources: fireplaces or wood-burning stoves

MANURE TEA—A QUICK, EFFECTIVE FERTILIZER

Soaking 3 pounds of steer or dairy manure in 5 gallons of water for 24 hours produces a fertilizer so rich it must be diluted for use on vegetables or annuals. Build a tripod (of 8-foot 2 x 2s) from which to suspend a burlap or cotton bag full of manure into a can or tub of just enough water to cover the manure. After about 24 hours, the liquid will be as black as dark coffee. Though a manure tea is less likely to burn plants than are dry fertilizers, at full strength it is still too strong for direct application. Before using, dilute it until it looks like weak tea. Err on the side of caution when diluting, as exact strength is hard to calculate.

The tea is most efficiently used on small beds or specific foundation plants. Spade the leftover leached-out manure into the garden or turn it into the compost pile.

RESOURCES FOR ORGANIC GARDENERS

The following mail-order nurseries and garden supply centers offer materials and seeds to organic gardeners through catalogs. Most of them are free; a few charge a fee, usually refunded with your first purchase. Also listed are specialists in predators and parasites of pests.

GARDEN SUPPLY SOURCES

Gardens Alive!
Natural Gardening Research Center
P. O. Box 149
Sunman, IN 47041
(812) 623-3800
Pest controls, equipment, fertilizers, some seeds

Harmony Farm Supply
P. O. Box 460
Graton, CA 95444
(707) 823-9125
Pest controls, equipment, fertilizers

Necessary Trading Co.
P. O. Box 305
Newcastle, VA 24127
Pest controls, equipment, fertilizers

Peaceful Valley Farm Supply
P. O. Box 2209

Grass Valley, CA 95945
(916) 272-4769
Pest controls, equipment, fertilizers, some seeds

Smith & Hawken
25 Corte Madera
Mill Valley, CA 94941
(415) 383-4415
Pest controls, equipment, seeds, nursery stock, soil amendments, fertilizers

SEED SUPPLIERS

Bountiful Gardens
19550 Walker Rd.
Willits, CA 95490
Cover crop and other seeds, legume inoculants

W. Atlee Burpee Co.
300 Park Ave.
Warminster, PA 18991
Cover crop and other seeds, legume inoculants

Nichols Garden Nursery
1190 N. Pacific Hwy.
Albany, OR 97321
Cover crop and other seeds, legume inoculants

Stokes Seed, Inc.
P. O. Box 548
Buffalo, NY 14240
Cover crop and other seeds, legume inoculants

Territorial Seed Co.
Box 27
Lorane, OR 97451
Cover crop and other seeds, legume inoculants

PEST CONTROL SPECIALISTS

Biosys
1057 East Meadow Circle
Palo Alto, CA 94303
(415) 856-9500
Predator nematodes

Mead's Resistant Predatory Mites
9093 Troxel Road
Chico, CA 95928
(916) 895-8125
Predator mites

Biological Control Services Program
California Department of Food and Agriculture
1220 N Street, Room A-149
Sacramento, CA 95814
Catalog of specialist suppliers of predators and parasites

APPLYING FERTILIZERS

Gardening is always more of an art than a science, but this is never so clear as when it comes time to fertilize. Ask 10 experts, get 10 answers . . . all of them with qualifications and stipulations that swiftly multiply the total creative possibilities.

Take heart: the basic problem is not that tough to solve. Add at least a small amount of nitrogen every year and plants will grow; everything else is fine tuning. The long-term goal should be to improve soil structure and balance pH by adding organic material with balanced fertilizer value. The reason for this approach is that whatever nutrients are in your soil become freely available when that soil has a proper ratio of solids, air, and moisture and when its pH is in the ideal range of 6.0 to 6.8.

In fact, one of the major claims of veteran organic gardeners is that year by year they spend less and less on fertilizer because perfectly structured, richly organic soil contains enough nutrients of its own.

The following recommendations offer three starting blocks for an annual program to get an unproductive garden up and running. A soil test gives you a head start, but observation of your plants can get you there, too. If testing or weak plants point to a deficiency (see page 20), begin with one of the recommendations in the third plan. If your plants are growing passably well, use one of the first two. All three plans are based on pounds of fertilizer per 1,000 square feet.

1. From Washington State University, here's an all-purpose formula for flower and/or vegetable beds with medium phosphorus and potassium, or for untested soils: N (4 pounds)–P (10 pounds)–K (6 pounds).

2. The University of Georgia offers this recipe for vegetable beds with medium phosphorus and potassium soils:

For heavy feeders, N (3 pounds)–P (4.5 pounds)–K (4.5 pounds).

For medium feeders, N (1.5 pounds)–P (2.3 pounds)–K (2.3 pounds).

For light feeders, N (0.75 pounds)–P (1.5 pounds)– K (1.5 pounds).

(See page 21 for lists of heavy, medium, and light feeders. See at right for measures of phosphorus and potassium content in soil.)

3. For those who have a soil test to guide them, Washington State University gives the following ratios (and rough totals):

If P/K are . . .	Use fertilizer ratio . . .
high/high	1:1:1 (20 lb. 10–10–10 or 30 lb. 6–8–4)
medium/high	1:1:1 (25 lb. 10–10–5 or 35 lb. 6–8–4)
low/high	1:3:1 (30 lb. 5–15–5)
high/medium	1:1:1 (20 lb. 10–10–10 or 30 lb. 6–8–4)
high/low	1:1:2 (22 lb. 10–10–20 + 4 lb. muriate of potash)
medium/low	1:1:2 (40 lb. 5–5–10 or 20 lb. 10–10–10 + 4 lb. muriate of potash)
low/medium	1:3:1 (40 lb. 5–15–10)
low/low	1:3:2 (40 lb. 5–15–10)

The totals given in parentheses are for commercial fertilizers, so organic equivalents need to be worked out. Where soil tests or plant performance show potassium and phosphorus are already medium to high, adding more will do no harm—but only nitrogen needs to be added right away.

Soil test values are as follows:

P: low, 0 to 5; medium, 5 to 10; high, 10+

K: low, 0 to 75; medium, 75 to 120; high, 120+

Fertilizer volumes are totals. If a combination of fertilizers were to be used, their contributions would have to be added together.

How to Calculate Fertilizer Volumes

Nitrogen, phosphorus, and potassium contents of fertilizers are given as percentages of the total weight. To calculate the amount of fertilizer available, multiply the number of pounds of material by the percentage of the nutrient in question.

For example: a 50-pound bag of fertilizer that is 5 percent nitrogen will have 2.5 pounds of nitrogen in it (50 x .05 = 2.5). Someone needing 3 pounds of nitrogen would have to use a bag plus 10 pounds of such a material. The following table will save you some arithmetic:

1% = 1 lb. of nutrient per 100 lb. of material
1.5% = 1 lb. of nutrient per 75 lb. of material
2% = 1 lb. of nutrient per 50 lb. of material
2.5% = 1 lb. of nutrient per 40 lb. of material
3% = 1 lb. of nutrient per 33 lb. of material
4% = 1 lb. of nutrient per 25 lb. of material
5% = 1 lb. of nutrient per 20 lb. of material
6% = 1 lb. of nutrient per 16.5 lb. of material
8% = 1 lb. of nutrient per 12.5 lb. of material
10% = 1 lb. of nutrient per 10 lb. of material

Note: familiar-brand packaged fertilizers list their nutrients as percentages available to plants within one growing season of application. Organic fertilizers list their nutrients as pure totals; the nutrients may take more than a year to become available to plants.

HOW TO CORRECT pH IN SOIL

Soils that are overly acidic or alkaline stunt plant growth either by inhibiting the plant's ability to take up nutrients—especially trace elements—or by making them so readily available that they become toxic to the plant.

Soils can be brought back into balance fairly quickly if they are not too far out of the ideal range of pH 6.0 to 6.8. Be sure to spade the material into the top 8 inches of soil, mixing thoroughly.

If the soil is mildly acidic (pH 5.5 to 6.0), add 30 to 50 pounds of limestone or 60 to 100 pounds of wood ashes per 1,000 square feet.

If it's moderately acidic (pH 5.0 to 5.5), add 60 to 100 pounds of limestone or 120 to 200 pounds of wood ashes per 1,000 square feet in two applications, one before turning the earth in early autumn and the next as early as possible in spring.

If it's highly acidic (pH 4.9 or less), double the rates again, dividing the applications over 2 years. If the soil is alkaline (pH 7.2 to 8.0), add soil sulfur at the rate of 10 to 20 pounds per 1,000 square feet. Iron sulfate is a poor alternative because it stains nearly everything it touches.

COMPOSTING

Turning green matter back into highly organic soil is no minor art, because there are several basic approaches—and for every one, the details vary according to local humidity, temperatures, and even local beliefs.

The progressive levels of intensity and commitment needed to turn green matter into organic soil are mulching, green manuring, sheet composting, cool composting, and hot composting.

The significant point to remember in all of these composting systems is that proper decomposition is the work of aerobic (oxygen-using) bacteria in the soil. That means the key component is moisture, which must be constant but never saturating. Get decomposing plant material too wet and anaerobic bacteria will take over, producing sewerlike smells of rotting plants.

One other general rule applies: Composting works better as a batch process than a continuous one. That is, once a pile is started it should be allowed to decompose fully without having to adjust to new material.

What to put in:

- lawn clippings
- soft leaves
- soft stalks and stems of annuals
- fruit pulp and skins (use garden culls, and perhaps kitchen waste, only in hot compost systems)
- highly organic earth

What to keep out:

- woody stalks (too slow to decompose)
- pet excrement (draws flies)
- meat waste (draws flies)

Mulching. The gardener puts down a layer of organic material to help retain moisture during a growing season. At the end of the growing season, the mulch is turned into the soil to continue decomposing.

Green manuring. A winter cover crop is turned into the soil in time for it to decompose before the next planting season begins—or else ground is left fallow for a cover crop to grow and be turned under before permanent plants are installed.

Sheet composting. This is not very different from green manuring: plant material grown elsewhere is spread in an even layer and then covered with earth. The layer decomposes between growing seasons.

Cool composting. This laissez-faire technique allows a pile of plant material to decompose haphazardly. Usually the process takes 2 years to complete.

Hot composting. "True" composting is hard work but produces the greatest amount of the most nutrient-rich humus of any system, because it transforms plant material back into earth in as few as 4 weeks and at the same time preserves the greatest possible proportion of nutrients. Incidentally, it usually takes several trials to get the right mix of materials for an active hot composting pile.

Mulching

A mulch is any material placed over the soil to reduce evaporation, to reduce or prevent weed growth, and to moderate soil temperature changes. Potential water savings from mulching are greatest in hot, dry climates. Weed control is effective anywhere. Soil temperatures are kept cooler during sun hours, warmer at night.

In green manuring, spade narrow slices of earth, turning under both roots and foliage. Chopping foliage fine beforehand speeds the process.

Mulches also prevent splashing of soil onto leaves (which in turn diminishes the development of some soilborne diseases). They also appear to make soil more attractive to earthworms, because of its improved moisture retention and more constant temperatures.

In the long term, they improve the organic content of soil, when spaded in after each growing season.

The most common organic mulches in the western United States are aged sawdust, ground tree bark, peat moss, and homemade compost. Straw, hay, conifer needles, and lawn clippings also enjoy wide use. Less common mulches include rice hulls, nut hulls, and cotton gin waste.

In tests by *Sunset's* garden editors, the winners for all-around performance were ground bark and compost. Aged sawdust finished a close third. Decorative bark performed least well (it decomposes very slowly, displaces easily, is not as efficient as others in retaining moisture, and is costly).

To be effective, most mulches should be 2 to 4 inches thick, the lighter ones 3 to 6 inches.

Here are a few cautions about mulches not mentioned on page 28 under "Fertilizers & Soil Amendments":

■ Lawn clippings should be spread to dry for a day or so, or they will cake together and breed flies.

■ Pine needles are acidic, so they should only be used around plants that thrive in those soils. Because they're coarse, they should be 6 inches deep.

■ Straw has few or no seeds, whereas hay has many that sprout into weeds.

■ Rice hulls and cotton gin waste are so light that they should be covered with another, heavier mulch.

Green Manuring & Sheet Composting

Green manuring is the end product of cover crops selected for their ability to improve soil. That is, a cover crop becomes green manure when spent plants are spaded into the soil in early spring, before summer plantings. It is the first resort of many organic gardeners who need to improve poor soil, because the effects are long lasting. It is not, however, a quick fix. Genuinely impoverished soils may need several years of cover crops and green manuring to be fully restored.

Green manuring is the court of first resort for garden soils that have been compacted during construction or otherwise pounded solid. In such situations, the technique has a double advantage: not only does it add organic matter, but it lets the roots loosen the soil as they grow. Even in iron-hard clays, rye grows so much root so fast that one long-time proponent calls it "the world's greatest shovel."

Sheet composting, too, involves digging a uniform layer of spent plants into the soil. The difference is that it uses plants grown elsewhere.

The advantage of green manuring, especially, is that you needn't move large amounts of material from one place to another. Some cover crops grow well enough to provide material for composting as well as some to be dug in as green manure.

The potential drawback to both methods is that they steal space from permanent plantings, a problem in small plots. But gardeners with ample space can plant parts of a developing garden with cover crops on a rotating cycle until all of it has benefited from their presence.

Here are some tips for choosing cover crops:

- Fava beans, vetch, wheat, rye, and clovers are common choices. All cover crops act as a sort of living mulch, choking out weeds and controlling erosion. And beans or grains produce edible crops as a bonus.

- Both fava beans and vetch are nitrogen-fixing crops, accumulating nitrogen in their roots and leaving a dose of it in the soil. If you grow them together, the favas can act as trellises up which the vetch climbs; the vetch helps keep favas from blowing over in the wind. Purple vetch is best for mild climates; hairy vetch or wooly pod vetch replaces it in cold-winter climes. If eye appeal is important, white clover can replace the fava-vetch mixture. Other peas and beans can substitute for favas if the crop is meant to be edible as well as a source of green manure.

- The extensive root systems of wheat and rye benefit soil structure, and their carbon content at maturity helps keep nitrogen from leaching out of the soil.

- It is not uncommon to interplant all of the foregoing as soils develop. Rye is sometimes planted alone for the first year in infertile soils, and mustard is a good cover crop for heavy or compacted soils.

- If you plant favas and/or clover, treat the crop with a legume inoculant to improve its nitrogen-fixing ability. Inoculants are available from seed companies and may be ordered along with your seed.

These and others of the best green manures are cool-season crops, planted in fall after the soil has cooled and then harvested, composted, or both while they are still succulent. In mild-winter areas October is the prime planting time. In cool, wet climates plant just before heavy autumn rains start. In cold climates plant 2 months before the first hard frost. (See plant selections on pages 74–94.)

Cool Composting

Cool composting is an easy option for gardeners with plenty of space and a corner of the garden that can be somewhat unsightly at all times.

In essence, you throw each year's worth of grass trimmings, fallen leaves, and spent plants onto a pile and leave them to their own devices for 2 years or more, until they are completely decomposed. This means there are always two piles going, and sometimes three.

Because little heat is generated by bacterial action, the material that goes in should exclude all food scraps (they will attract breeding flies), all weeds (the seeds will sprout sooner or later), and all diseased plant materials (the disease organism will remain active).

Purists will also argue that most of the nitrogen is lost from material composted this way, leaving only a soil conditioner.

Hot Composting

Hot composting pays big dividends in the form of high volumes of excellent soil conditioner with good fertilizer value every 4 to 8 weeks during the growing season. Take a hint, however, from those who went "back to the earth" and plunged into organic gardening in the 1960s. They'll tell you that hot composting just plain wore them out with its incessant demands on time and muscle power. The problem was that they wanted to cover the world with compost overnight, so let nothing green escape the heap.

In fact, because it's a batch process, composting can be an episodic activity—transforming perhaps just 1 cubic yard's worth of a winter cover crop, or the last great flurry of summer growth—or maybe one of each.

The following long list of conditions for success helps explain why many start yet stumble.

- At the outset, a compost pile should be 4 to 6 feet deep and at least 1 yard square. Any shallower or smaller, and the center of the pile cannot heat up enough for aerobic bacteria to flourish. Any deeper, and it compresses itself too much for proper aeration.

- Bins or piles should be no more than 5 feet wide for ease of access and turning.

- The temperature in the pile must rise to 140°F, but not soar much above that. Mild climates with some summer rain are the easiest ones in which to maintain those temperatures. Desert climates are toughest because of both heat and dryness.

- While the pile is working, it should always be about as wet as a moist sponge. Any drier, and no bacteria flourish. Any wetter, and foul-smelling anaerobic types dominate. (Test the pile just as you would a baking cake: poke a dry stick into the middle. The tip should come out moist and sweet smelling.)

In dry climates, the pile may need to be watered every third or fourth day and should have a concave top to funnel moisture inward. In rainy climates, a mounded pile may shed enough water by its shape alone, or it may need a covering of plastic film to maintain the correct moisture level.

- To keep enough oxygen at the core for aerobic bacteria to flourish, turn and loosen the pile with a pitchfork at regular intervals. If the material is chopped very fine and the pile tends to stay very moist, turn every third or fourth day. If the material is coarser and drier, turn once a week or even every other week.

When turning, move material from the cool

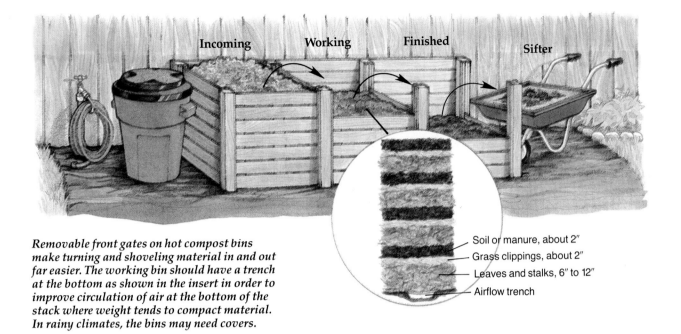

Incoming   Working   Finished   Sifter

Soil or manure, about 2"
Grass clippings, about 2"
Leaves and stalks, 6" to 12"
Airflow trench

Removable front gates on hot compost bins make turning and shoveling material in and out far easier. The working bin should have a trench at the bottom as shown in the insert in order to improve circulation of air at the bottom of the stack where weight tends to compact material. In rainy climates, the bins may need covers.

toward the warm center so that the whole pile decomposes fairly evenly.

Getting Started. Once a hot pile is started, it should be allowed to decompose without new material being added. For this reason, most composters use a three-part bin system: dry new material waiting to compost in one, working material in a second, and finished material waiting to go into the garden in the third.

To get the first working pile under way, do the following:

■ Gather separate stacks of green, moist, highly nitrogenous material (lawn clippings are ideal); firmer, drier material (oak or other tree leaves, for example); and organic earth. The nitrogenous material feeds bacteria. The firmer material assures airways throughout the pile. The organic earth provides bacteria to work on.

■ For swifter results, chop any thick stalks or large leaves into smaller bits, ideally about an inch in diameter. (The greater the surface, the more quickly bacteria can work; but there are practical limits, as larger material assures airways throughout the pile.)

■ Put down a thick layer of the coarse material, then add separate, thinner layers of the other two. Repeat the layers, always in the same sequence, until the pile is at least 4 feet deep. The exact depth of the layers will depend on local climate conditions. As a starting point, try 6 to 12 inches of the coarser, drier material and 2 inches each of the moist material and rich organic earth.

If you have no ready supply of organic earth, buy a bag of compost mixed with manure from a garden supply center to start with. Subsequent batches can draw on the first for organic soil rich in the right sort of bacteria.

Following are several designs of composting bins for projects or properties of various sizes.

BINS FOR COMPOSTING

People with large gardens have the space and volume of debris to put up large, permanent bins of the sort shown in the drawing above. Most of us have less space and less to compost. Smaller spaces also dictate that the bins be inoffensive to the eye, because there's nowhere to hide them. On page 42 are one store-bought and two homemade solutions to this common problem. All three are practical first and foremost, but also take appearance into account.

Few of us have so much garden space that we can allow a compost pile to look as casually untidy as it might on a farm. If appearance is not a big concern, the easiest and cheapest compost container is a 6- to 9-foot length of chicken wire formed into a circle and fastened with bits of wire. When you want to work the pile, just lift the wire off and set it to one side, then shovel the pile back into it. Invert the stack when you do this by shoveling the old top material in first and the bottom material in last.

A Store-bought Solution. Several manufacturers produce sturdy plastic compost bins. The best are modest in expense but durable and well designed. Features to look for are a volume of just over 1 cubic yard, bottom doors large enough to get into with a shovel for turning and removal, and easy disassemblage for flat storage when not in use.

A Simple Bin. Made of 1-x-2 redwood, poultry wire, and redwood lath, this bin holds exactly 1 cubic yard. Its four sides are held together with large hooks and eyes. To turn a pile, the designer recommends taking the bin apart from around the pile and setting it up again next to it. Then the pile is forked into the repositioned bin, with the top layer now on the bottom. The hook-and-eye system permits flat storage between seasons.

An Attractive Space Saver. Stacked, this three-part system totals 1 cubic yard but composts smaller batches efficiently in a minimum of space. It's made of redwood 2 x 2s and half-inch wire mesh. Each section is 30 inches square and 16 inches deep; one extra panel serves as both lid and sifter. Once the first batch is ready, the sections decompose in turn, the bottom one finishing while the middle works at peak activity and the top fills with new material. As decomposition is reached in the bottom section, it's emptied and placed on top of the stack to receive new matter. Each section should have layers of coarse matter, fine matter, and active humus, just as larger piles do.

French intensive garden at Fetzer Vineyards in Mendocino County, California, is both a laboratory and a public demonstration of the basic techniques. Mounded beds of highly organic earth, drip irrigation, and close plantings of wildly mixed species characterize it.

FRENCH INTENSIVE

Everything flourishes in mounded beds. Plants nestle cheek-by-jowl rather than marching in neat rows. The secret lies underground: soil enriched by heavy infusions of rotted manure, bonemeal, and other natural sources of nutrient, to the point at which no amount of roots could exhaust the supply. It is organic gardening carried to its logical limit.

The system is called sometimes French Intensive, sometimes Biodynamic. Used in Europe for generations, it was brought to California in the 1960s and introduced to the Garden Project at the University of California at Santa Cruz. You mound beds to make a body of soil that warms quickly, drains well, and takes in air easily. Mounding also accommodates the quantities of new material you add to build a balanced soil. Before planting add enough organic material so that soil texture and fertility constantly improve. As soil improves, it becomes easier to "make the beds."

Close-crowded plantings shade the soil, reducing moisture loss and preventing temperature extremes. This encourages the fast, steady growth that produces tender, full-flavored vegetables and plentiful blossoms. The shade also reduces weeds and helps keep soil from crusting. Once low-growing plants cover a bed, you rarely need to weed or cultivate.

Beds can be any size or shape you wish, but rectangles are easiest to build and care for. They should be narrow enough to be cultivated from pathways on either side, so as not to get compacted by foot traffic.

For ornamentals, a dizzying mix is much practiced to minimize pest damage. For vegetables, you can divide a bed into sections and plant each with a different crop, so long as they have compatible growing needs. Seeds need to be watered more often than plants, so most people don't try to sow seeds and transplant into the same bed.

What follows is the basic sequence for establishing a French Intensive garden:

1. Divide the area to be planted into beds running north-south. Use stakes and string to outline them.

Double digging is the essence of preparing soil for a French intensive garden, but it is a useful idea for every gardener. Start by digging one row to a spade's depth and putting the soil (1) to one side. Dig and turn the soil of that row down another spade's depth (2). Move to a second row and turn the top section's soil (3) into the first hole (1); then dig and turn the next layer down (4). Continue the width of the bed, finally putting the top soil from row 1 in the last hole. The final step is to mix in organic material and form a mounded bed.

2. Beds for plants that need vertical support—beans, cucumbers, peas, tomatoes—should be a foot and a half wide. Make beds for other plants wider, but narrow enough so that you can easily reach the center from either side (usually from 3 to 5 feet wide).

3. Double-dig the whole bed as shown in the illustration above. Blend in compost or other organic matter and sand as needed to create a soil approximately equal in compost, sand, and original garden soil. Leave the surface rough for 2 to 5 days, to air it out. Then break up the clods and work to a fine texture, keeping the mounded shape. If you plan to sow seeds on a mound, save enough soil in a wheelbarrow to cover them.

4. Next, sprinkle on a thin layer of bonemeal, an inch or two of rotten manure, and, if available, a dusting of wood ash. Turn these materials into the top 3 to 6 inches of the bed, depending on how deep rooted the crop to be planted is. Then rake the soil into a smooth mound.

5. Soak the soil with a gentle spray the day before planting. As plants mature, water deeply enough to soak the whole root area and often enough to keep the top 2 inches moist. (Most such gardens of any size have permanent drip systems to conserve both water and the gardener's energy.)

6. Spacing between plants is important, and transplanting gives you more control over that factor than sowing does. However, you will have to start some crops from seed because they do not transplant well. (For example, celery, coles, eggplant, leeks, lettuce, onions, and peppers transplant readily but beets, bush beans, carrots, parsnips, dwarf peas, radishes, and rutabagas do not.)

7. Set both edible and ornamental plants at intervals so that their outer leaves will just touch as they approach mature size. (For instance, lettuce should be about 8 inches apart, cabbage about 15.) Plant in staggered lines across the beds rather than in straight rows.

COMMUNITY COMPOSTING

In dozens of small communities across the United States residents have found community composting to be the perfect solution to the common problems of too little space and time.

Larger cities appear to find that logistical and other problems require more complex solutions, but that community composting can be a major means of cutting down the amount of solid waste going into ever-harder-pressed landfills.

Residential communities offering such programs (in combination with other recycling programs) have reduced solid wastes going to landfills by more than 40 percent. Some midsized cities have managed reductions approaching 25 percent. This is not small potatoes in an era when solid waste disposal has become politically charged ("Not In My Backyard"), logistically difficult (sites 100 miles and more away), and expensive (costing from $115 to $120 a ton for gathering and disposal).

Well-managed composting programs return organic matter to tillable soil and can recover at least part of their cost by selling the compost.

In some small towns the government can simply set aside space at the municipal landfill for residents to dump autumn leaves, prunings, and other garden debris. The disposal company manages the material and sells finished compost to homeowners and landscape gardeners, recouping some of the cost while delaying the day when the landfill site will be exhausted.

Another approach tried with some success is for the city to contract with a major local nursery to set up and manage the program on land provided rent free by the city. The nursery sells the supply to both private gardeners and landscaping companies.

Another possibility for a small city is to run a collecting and composting organization separately from its regular disposal service. Municipalities with enough government structure to have a fleet of dump trucks or other suitable trucks can "borrow" them from their regular departments for curbside recycling of garden wastes at peak seasons during the year. The obvious times are spring, when the first wave of cleanup and planting takes place, and autumn. Such an effort takes a forceful public information program in order for the material to be at curbside when it is supposed to be there, and in a condition that makes for efficient pickup by city crews. It also takes a dis-

posal site of some size to handle the sudden influx, though the site may be open all year for citizen use.

Incentives never hurt. One is to charge citizens a lower fee for dumping compostable material at a designated site than for general garbage dumped into the landfill. Another is to offer some amount of free compost in return for a certain amount of raw material.

Larger cities generate too much material over too large an area for one single program to solve the whole problem. Seattle, Washington, has taken a double-barreled approach.

The city disposal service maintains a composting site. Homeowners can pay for curbside pickup or they can transport their own garden waste to neighborhood transfer points, from whence city trucks haul it to the central site. The city sells finished compost from this program to landscapers and nurseries.

Simultaneously, Seattle's government has tried to transfer much of the responsibility for recycling plant debris from home gardens to individual homeowners by teaching them how to compost. The city backs up this carrot with a stick: a 1989 ordinance forbids the disposal of garden waste in city landfills.

The Seattle training program for residents has gone through two stages and is now in a third.

First the city set up neighborhood demonstration centers where volunteers took garden debris from people and showed them how to compost it.

After all the volunteer centers had been overwhelmed by "donated" material, the city contracted with a local gardening organization called Seattle Tilth to teach a core population of composters. Each trainee was required in turn to donate 40 hours of community service in the form of training still more home gardeners in the art of turning leaves back into soil.

Finally the city bought thousands of manufactured compost bins and offered them—plus training from a well-versed composter working under contract—free to all who asked. This program has been designed to continue until at least a quarter of Seattle's households are involved.

Community composting centers must be well managed. Typical large-scale composting systems use a skip-loader or front-loader to work windrows about 5 feet high and 12 to 15 feet wide during the year the material is decomposing. In addition they need a screening and bagging setup if they are to sell compost to recoup some of the operating costs.

MANAGING PESTS & DISEASES

Yeccch, bugs! is a standard American response to creeping things in the garden. Is it justified? Well, yeccch and no. . . . In the first place, some creeping things are predators of other creeping things. In the second, quite a few others are neither helpful nor harmful. Finally, the job of many "pests" is to ensure survival of the fittest, which means they attack weak plants. But even the most dedicated proponents of organic gardening admit that gaining control of pests and diseases is slower and less complete than it is with synthetic chemicals. What control a gardener achieves comes over a span of seasons. "Integrated pest management" has become something of a buzz phrase. By definition it means combining predators, plant selection, and other biological methods to make life hard for the bad guys. The first important step toward control is to achieve healthy, fertile soil. It—literally—gives rise quickly to healthy plants that are better able than fragile ones to withstand diseases and pests. Even more important, however, is your selection of plants. Interplanting susceptible plants with others that discourage or at least do not attract pests is also useful for disease and pest resistance. Rotating crops is another help. (The final chapter of this book offers a selection of plants, some resistant to pests, some not. Also see "Staying a Step Ahead of Trouble," pages 22–23, for some suggestions for crop rotation.) However, healthy soil and a sagacious planting scheme may take several years to develop. In the meantime, the battle against pests and diseases must be joined at the first trumpet call and waged unrelentingly, with all weapons at hand. The first part of this chapter covers the weaponry of straightforward war: predators and parasites, organic sprays and powders. These should be augmented by pinching fingers and stamping feet, and also by traps and shields. Keeping the garden free of downed leaves is every bit as important as sprays and hand-picking. And it must be admitted that the most dedicated organic gardener will face slower going if surrounded by either wildlands or nonorganically gardening neighbors. Wildlands will harbor an unending supply of pests that are neutral there but calamitous in a garden, especially in one full of edibles. Nonorganic gardeners unwittingly chase many of their pests onto what is, for the pests, a veritable game refuge. Heeding the admonition to "know thine enemy" means that this chapter also contains a brief rogues' gallery of familiar and damaging garden pests and diseases, noting the plants they harm most and the controls that harm them most. Though this list runs to more than 35 entries, it is very short indeed. As long ago as the 1950s, the U. S. Department of Agriculture recognized more than 10,000 plant pests. And new counts keep upping the figure.

LIVING ALLIES

Gardeners are not the only earthly beings anxious to dispatch aphids, earwigs, snails, and other pests. A whole panoply of allies are to be found among insects, reptiles, amphibians, birds, and even other mammals—for instance, bats.

"Around here," the director of a showplace organic garden once said to a journalist, "we don't kill anything until we know what it does." Not bad words to live and let live by. Many of the insects, reptiles, and other traditionally unlovely creatures in a garden are on the gardener's side. Be advised, however, that the most warriorlike of them will not provide a quick fix. In fact, predators will not gather until a pest population becomes abundant enough to provide a feast, and will not stay on once the plate is empty.

This can be a most discouraging reflection when a prized plant is under attack—one reason for the go-slow approach to planting described under "Setting a Strategy" on pages 8–9. Sometimes leaving a much-eaten plant in the ground for a few days is wisest, on the chance that it will attract predators of whatever is feeding on it. Your first reaction will be to get rid of the host plant immediately, but observe it before you act. If ladybird beetles are gathering around an aphid-infested annual, for example, they will stick around to keep the pests from dispersing to other plants in the garden.

Several predator insects—particularly ladybird beetles and praying mantises—can be bought at nurseries or by mail order. But most people who have tried this tactic have been dissatisfied with the results. Ladybird beetles move on as soon as they are released, because they are genetically programmed to spread out to guarantee food for all. Mantises are more decorative than voracious, and are slow to reproduce if they reproduce at all.

BRACONID WASPS

Small (half-inch) to tiny (aphid-sized) wasps, braconids lay eggs that parasitize the larvae of pests. Because they are so small, most go unnoticed by gardeners. Several species are natives; others have been imported as pest controls for farm crops.

Prey: Nymphs of most braconids feed on aphids, scales, many caterpillars (including tomato hornworms), and the larvae of some flies. One species attacks leafrollers. Other braconids—cabbageworm parasite, pea aphid parasite, and woolly aphid parasite—control the insects they're named for.

Notes: In most cases a wasp injects just one egg into a pest or attaches one to its skin, but some species deposit multiple eggs that develop into cocoons (as shown). Some increasingly effective species were populous before the advent of chemical insecticides but nearly disappeared before developing a resistance to allow their resurgence.

Sources: mail-order firms (see page 36), nature

BUGS

One identifying trait of true bugs—such as assassin bugs (shown), big-eyed bugs, damsel bugs, and wheelbugs—is that they pierce their victims and suck fluids from them. Most are about half an inch long and quick moving. Bugs are among the more effective predators.

Prey: Adults and nymphs feed on aphids, leafhoppers, small caterpillars, thrips, and spider mites. Adult big-eyed bugs are an important predator of lygus bugs; adult damsel bugs also control lygus. Pirate bugs, among the smallest, are effective against thrips and spider mites.

Notes: Big-eyed bugs have big eyes; they are buff colored or darker. Damsel bugs are tan to gray with enlarged front legs used to grasp prey. Assassin bugs have red abdomens. Pirate bugs are checkered white and black or brown and black and have quite prominent beaks, in a family of prominent beaks.

Sources: nature

EARTHWORMS

Earthworms are not predators or parasites, but they're beneficial for other reasons. They earn their good reputation as adjunct soil conditioners and fertilizer enhancers. A healthy crop of worms is very nearly an absolute sign of healthy, biologically active soil with proper structure to provide oxygen and moisture to plant roots. The most active processors of compost are called Red Wiggler (sometimes Red Hybrid); night crawlers are also common.

Prey: Earthworms are not predators.

Notes: The digestive activities of earthworms increase available nitrates, calcium, phosphorus, and potassium in the soils in which they feed. They will not live in fresh manure or fresh compost, but thrive only when soils are rich in well-rotted amounts of one or both—preferably when applied as a mulch.

To establish worms in a bed, dig 6-inch-wide holes 4 to 5 feet apart and as deep as the topsoil goes; fill these with rich soil, mixing in worms in the process. Cover the bed with mulch.

Sources: nature, some nurseries, mail-order firms (see page 36, but may not survive in unfavorable soils and climates)

GROUND BEETLES

Ground beetles are a family ranging in size from pea-sized to more than an inch. Most are black or blue-black, but some have green or other metallic sheens on their wing covers. Predator members of the group rival ladybird beetles in effectiveness against insect pests.

Prey: Adults and larvae feed on a wide variety of ground-dwelling pests; some even feed on snails and slugs.

Notes: Ground beetles hide in the soil or under debris during the day and feed at night. Calasoma beetles (shown) secrete an irritant, so they should be handled only with gloves.

Sources: nature

HONEYBEES

The great pollenizer is the gardener's friend for just that reason. Like the earthworm, it's no predator but is included here as a reminder that it is lethally affected by many insect control measures.

Prey: The honeybee is not a predator.

Notes: Honeybees are extremely susceptible to many sprays, even organic ones. Apply summer oils only from late evening through early morning, during moderate temperatures (low temperatures slow evaporation; high ones extend the bees' period of activity). *Bacillus thuringiensis*, lime-sulfur, and sulfur are safe at any time.

Sources: beekeepers, nature

ICHNEUMON WASPS

Also incorrectly called "ichneumon flies," these insects parasitize a variety of caterpillars with their eggs. A distinct color spot on the leading edges of their wings identifies the group, which ranges from tiny to more than an inch long and may be brown, red, or black with variable markings.

Prey: The wasps attack beet webworms, corn earworms, armyworms, codling moth caterpillars, and other caterpillars. They will also attack bees.

Notes: Females have a long egg-laying tube at the tip of the abdomen. Eggs are deposited in host caterpillars, and the larvae usually develop internally. Some species have been imported as specific parasites of agricultural pests.

Sources: nature

LACEWINGS

Lacewing adults (shown on left) are one of nature's most beautiful insects, but their larvae (shown on right) look something like miniature alligators and have a temperament to match. The larvae are also known as "aphid lions."

Prey: The larvae suck fluids from aphids and spider mites.

Notes: The adults feed primarily on nectar and honeydew but will also attack aphids, especially in spring. Eggs are attached to leaves and stems by long silken threads and hatch as larvae throughout spring and summer. Larvae are identifiable by their long, sickle-shaped, hollow mandibles.

Sources: nature throughout western United States, mail-order firms (see page 36)

LADYBIRD BEETLES

Ladybird beetles—ladybugs to most of us—have the great advantage of being cute if you don't look too closely, which increases their survival rate and thus effectiveness. The family is extensive, but most are similar enough in appearance to be recognized without trouble. (Two of its members are pests; see the Mexican bean beetle and spotted cucumber beetle under "A Rogues' Gallery" beginning on page 56.)

Prey: Adults (shown on left) and larvae (shown on right) feed on aphids, mealybugs, scales, and spider mites.

Notes: Wing covers are almost always spotted and range in color from rosy pink to rusty brown. An adult female needs to consume 100 aphids before laying eggs. She must have two aphids per day per egg laid (which she deposits on the undersides of leaves, usually near aphid colonies). A single female may consume 3,400 aphids and lay 1,700 eggs as her life's work. There are one to three generations per year. The black-and-yellow larvae are more active feeders than the adults.

Sources: some nurseries, mail-order firms (see page 36), nature

PRAYING MANTISES

Even the most ardent of organic gardeners concede that praying mantises are of minor help in pest control. However, they are the showiest of the benign insects and thus make a convincing demonstration to youngsters of how biological control works in an organic garden.

Prey: Mantises consume aphids, primarily.

Notes: Will eat other benign insects as readily as pests. Tend not to reproduce if introduced into a garden rather than arriving naturally. Overwinter in egg cases attached to stems or house siding and hatch in early summer. Become adult by early autumn; there is one generation per year.

Sources: some nurseries, mail-order firms (see page 36), nature

ROBBER FLIES

This group of large flies contains several masters of disguise. Some of them look much like small bumblebees, others like wasps, and some like flies. Bulging eyes, a long, tapering, hairy body, and long legs are the markers of all members of the species.

Prey: Robber flies are fairly indiscriminate feeders.

Notes: Both larval and adult stages are predaceous.

Sources: nature

SPIDERS

Spiders have all sorts of bad habits. They spin webs where people can walk into them face first. They move indoors without invitation. A very few bite, leaving itchy welts or worse. Against all of that must be balanced the fact that they are active predators in the garden. Of the hundreds of kinds, the daddy longlegs is one of the least irritating to people and the most voracious consumers of insects, but jumping spiders (shown), crab spiders, and many others are likewise useful. Spiders' only weakness as predators is their lack of numbers.

Prey: Spiders are indiscriminate feeders.

Notes: Be wary of black widows (shiny black with a red hourglass on the abdomen) and brown violin spiders (matte brown with a darker brown violin-shaped mark on the abdomen), the two most dangerously poisonous spiders on the North American continent.

Sources: nature

SYRPHID FLIES

One of a loosely defined group called "hover flies" for their helicopterlike flying abilities, syrphids look like small wasps. Both larval maggots and adults are close to half an inch long.

Prey: Wrinkly green or brown syrphid maggots feed on aphids.

Notes: Long, white, pebbly eggs of syrphids are often laid in aphid colonies. Adults feed on nectar and honeydew from flowers.

Sources: nature

TACHINID FLIES

Tachinids (or sweat bees) belong, like syrphids, to the hover fly group. But they are much more industrious predators than their cousins and more variable in appearance, imitating several bees and wasps.

Prey: They feed on tent caterpillars, cutworms, zebra caterpillars, alfalfa loopers, squash bugs, stinkbugs, and sawflies.

Notes: Dark, bristly, bumblebeelike or wasplike tachinids frequently lay their eggs on the skins of caterpillars, especially tent caterpillars and cutworms.

Sources: nature

BIRDS, BATS, TOADS & OTHER SOMETIME ALLIES

Many of the small creatures that inhabit even city gardens consume insects with ravenous appetites yet arouse the unjustified animosity of gardeners.

Bats, birds, lizards, frogs, toads—even moles and gophers—all feed on insects. There are just two problems. First, they don't always discriminate between the insects you want to keep around and those you'd love to do away with. Second, they may be as much or more interested in your plants as a source of nutrition. Well, maybe there are three problems, if you count the way you may feel about their looks or some of their social habits.

Bats are particularly voracious predators of insects, and they can be encouraged to nest in the eaves of a building. (Sometimes they cannot be discouraged from it.) They eat exactly what is put before them. Examination of the stomach contents of bats in scores of regions has shown an almost exact cross-section of the insect population of the place and time. If the available diet is mostly beneficial insects, tough luck to your organic garden.

The other problem with bats is their susceptibility to rabies.

Toads, overall, are more agreeable company in a garden, and almost as hearty of appetite as bats. If you come across one burrowed into a shady spot, make it welcome—but don't expect miracles. Being groundbound and slow to get off the dime, they have a narrower range of prey than do winged creatures; but it also means they have a better chance of catching pests than catching the more agile beneficials.

In the best of circumstances a typical garden will not support a large toad population, and they are not likely to stick around at all where there are cats.

Lizards are about as valuable as toads. The kinds that are welcome are more numerous and wider ranging than toads, but they're also smaller and eat less.

Which brings us to birds.

Frustrated gardeners watching their ripening fruit feed robins, cedar waxwings, and starlings before it feeds them may wonder if there is any good in birds at all.

Some birds, of course, are almost entirely insectivorous: flycatchers, swallows, vireos, warblers, creepers, nuthatches, and woodpeckers among them. But even the pure insectivores are a mixed blessing because—like bats—they take the table the way it is set. In fact, they probably eat more beneficial insects than pests, because the beneficials are out hunting at the same time the birds are while the pests are hiding in the ground, in fruit, or on the undersides of leaves.

Birds that wreak the greatest destruction in gardens of edibles are blackbirds, robins, and starlings. Crows and magpies also eat garden fruit. But even these species are helpful now and again. Robins are among nature's most efficient predators of the codling moth. Starlings have done at least one good deed: they decimated a major infestation of gypsy moths in Massachussets in the 1950s.

Netting over trees and berry baskets or other shields over low growers will at least diminish the fee these species exact for their occasional help.

Amazing as it might seem, gophers and moles like to feed on beetle grubs in the soil. However, their achievements in this area do not come near to balancing the amount of vegetation they destroy.

ORGANIC SPRAYS & DUSTS

Integrated pest management is not all waiting around for predators to respond to your dinner invitations. Several organic sprays and powders can be unleashed on pests at will. But they are not uniformly effective against all the insects they control. With one exception, their toxicity to warm-blooded mammals is low or nonexistent, but several may be harmful to beneficial insects. These sprays break down quickly in soil and do not store in plant tissues, so they may have to be used repeatedly against persistent pests. To be cost effective they should be applied only to affected plants, not used as blanket sprays. The list offered here is not long, but the materials on it are well proven. Some organic gardeners wax enthusiastic about other materials, ranging from diatomaceous earth to garlic sprays to powders or sprays of ground insects. Controlled tests have cast doubt on their effectiveness, however.

BACILLUS THURINGIENSIS

Not a spray in the sense of the others but rather a related group of bacteria, *Bacillus thuringiensis*—BT for short—ranks among the most effective of organic controls for caterpillars. Special strains battle other pests. Each strain is blended into an inert host material, usually a wettable powder, to be activated according to instructions and applied as a spray. (*BT* is sold under trademarked names including Thuricide, Dipel, and Biological Worm Spray.)

Controls: most caterpillars, including tomato hornworms and those harmful to cole crops; (*BT* San Jose) Colorado potato beetles; (*BT* kurstaki) sod webworms; (*BT* israelensis) mosquitoes

Notes: BT is harmless to all creatures but target pests. It's most effective on young larvae, so should be applied as soon as first caterpillar damage appears. Does not reproduce, so it must be reapplied periodically according to instructions. *BT* takes 1 to 3 days to kill worms, but they usually stop feeding as soon as they begin ingesting it.

Sources: nurseries, mail-order firms (see page 36)

COPPER SULFATE

The most common of a group of copper compounds is a general-purpose fungicide and bactericide. A form that mixes in lime has long been known as "Bordeaux mixture," because it was first applied to vineyards there.

Controls: fireblight, peach leaf curl, shot-hole diseases; (Bordeaux mixture) mildew

Notes: Bordeaux mixture must be made afresh for each use; it cannot be kept because it is chemically unstable.

Sources: nurseries, mail-order firms (see page 36)

DORMANT OIL SPRAYS

Mineral and petroleum oils have been effective members of the organic gardener's arsenal since the 1780s but are comparatively little used. They are most effective against insect eggs. Those sold as dormant oils can be sprayed only on woody plants, and only while the plants are dormant (*see also* summer oils, lime-sulfur).

Controls: leaf roller eggs, aphids (eggs, nymphs, and adults), scales (eggs and adults), mites (eggs and adults)

Application: Spray during dormant season only, but not when temperature is below 40°F or above 90°F. Must be diluted with water.

Notes: Dormant oils will severely burn foliage if applied during the growing season. They can be diluted to half strength with water for use after leaves appear, but summer oils are a still better idea. They are not harmful to many beneficial insects and are nonhazardous to humans. They last indefinitely on the shelf after opening.

Sources: nurseries, mail-order firms (see page 36)

LIME-SULFUR

Technically calcium polysulfide, lime-sulfur does double duty as a fungicide-bactericide and an insecticide.

Controls: (fungicide-bactericide) peach leaf curl, powdery mildew, various leaf spots; (insecticide) scales, thrips, some mites

Notes: Calcium polysulfide also helps open up tightly knit soils by binding together clay particles. It is sometimes used to improve drainage in septic leach fields.

Sources: nurseries, mail-order firms (see page 36)

PYRETHRUM

An extract of a species of chrysanthemum, pyrethrum is most toxic to the larger beetles and caterpillars that feed on foliage. It also gives the satisfaction of swift control; affected insects usually die within minutes. Sunlight breaks down the compound rapidly, usually within a day, so repeated sprays may be necessary.

Controls: pickleworms, aphids, leafhoppers, harlequin bugs, cabbageworms, Mexican bean beetles, flea beetles, flies, squash bugs

Notes: To be effective, it must be mixed with an activator or synergist (such as piperonyl butoxide or piperonyl cyclonene); the spray must contact the pest directly. It is toxic to fish and is not effective against mites.

Sources: nurseries, mail-order firms (see page 36)

ROTENONE

An extract from the roots of certain South American plants, rotenone is most toxic to chewing insects. It is one of the few organic pesticides that require a 1- to 3-day interval between application and harvest when used on edibles.

Controls: Colorado potato beetles, Mexican bean beetles, Japanese beetles, flea beetles, cucumber beetles, spittlebugs, aphids, potato beetles, some mites, carpenter ants, cabbageworms, cabbage loopers, fleas

Application: Rotenone is commercially available as either a dust or a spray.

Notes: Rotenone is extremely toxic to fish and other cold-blooded creatures, as well as to hogs. It's ineffective against spider mites and soil insects. It is non-toxic to bees. Read the label carefully, especially for use on edible plants.

Sources: nurseries, mail-order firms (see page 36)

RYANIA

Ryania is a plant extract, most frequently used on apples and pears to control codling moth.

Controls: codling moths, Oriental fruit moths, potato aphids, onion thrips, corn earworms

Notes: Does not harm beneficial insects. It is sometimes formulated with diatomaceous earth.

Sources: rather few, usually specialty mail-order firms

SABADILLA

Sabadilla is one of the plant extracts toxic to insects.

Controls: armyworms, Harlequin bugs, stinkbugs, cucumber beetles, leafhoppers, cabbage loopers, blister beetles

Notes: Sabadilla breaks down quickly in sunlight. Can be used on food crops one day before gathering.

Sources: rather few, usually specialty mail-order firms

SOAP

Insect soap spray is available commercially or you can make your own. Homemade sprays (3 tablespoons of kitchen soap flakes or 3 to 6 tablespoons of liquid dishwashing soap to 1 gallon of water) are not quite as effective but work to some extent. Do not use detergents (which may not be effective) or laundry soaps (which may be too caustic for your plants).

Controls: mites, aphids, leafhoppers, scale larvae, pear psylla, greenhouse thrips, whiteflies

Notes: Spray affected plants until they are dripping wet. Soaps are strictly contact insecticides, working primarily by penetrating the protective waxy covering of most insects but in some cases through a direct effect on their nervous systems. With homemade sprays, spray only a small part of the plant to see how well it resists damage.

Sources: nurseries, home manufacture

SULFUR

Elemental sulfur is one of the most ancient weapons of gardeners and is more useful against diseases than many of the others. Additionally, it is an essential trace element for human health.

Controls: (mildewcide/fungicide) downy mildew, powdery mildew, scab, brown rot, botrytis molds; (insecticide) spider mites, aphids, leafhoppers, greenhouse thrips

Application: Can be applied as a finely ground powder or as a spray made from a wettable powder.

Notes: Avoid application when temperatures exceed 90°F, or within 4 weeks of using summer or other oils. There is a high risk of damage to melons and other cucurbits and to apricots, so don't use it on them. Do not use just prior to harvest of vegetables you plan to can (it could produce sulfur dioxide in the sealed containers, causing them to burst). Sulfur can be used on canned fruits or berries without this risk, and on all edibles eaten fresh, dried, or frozen.

Sources: nurseries, mail-order firms (see page 36)

SUMMER OILS

Like dormant oils, summer oils are distilled mineral oils. The difference is that they are distilled at lower temperatures, so they evaporate more quickly. As a result they can be used on plants during the foliage season with little or no fear of leaf burning. The lighter the oil, the less the risk. However, even the lightest oils may be used only on woody plants. These oils work against insects and their eggs by smothering them or by interfering with membrane functions.

Controls: scales, aphids, mealybugs, mites; also whitefly larvae, greenhouse thrips, leafhoppers

Application: Water before spraying; stressed plants could suffer burn. Spray when temperatures will remain under 90°F for the next 24 hours (if conditions are marginal, halve the strength of the oil).

Notes: Avoid spraying tender tip growth; do not use on azaleas, blue spruce, Japanese holly, Japanese maple, photinia, Savin juniper, smoke tree, walnut, or any other plant listed on the warning label. The shelf life of oils is virtually infinite.

Sources: nurseries, mail-order firms (see page 36)

A ROGUES' GALLERY

Of the thousands upon thousands of insects that will stop for a bite of something in your garden, only a handful are serious, long-term nuisances. However, they make up for the rest. The list that follows is aimed mostly at helping vegetable gardeners cope with insects that steal food from their tables, but it also includes some of the most troublesome pests for ornamentals.

Snails and slugs rank at or near the top of the list of general pests—the ones that feed on just about every plant people enjoy owning. Earwigs and grasshoppers are not far behind. This "big four" also have in common that their adult forms do all the damage and are usually the only stage gardeners encounter as they go about their chores. Aphids, mealybugs, and scales form a related trio, almost as familiar as the "big four" and almost as indiscriminate in their choice of plants to attack. However, with the exception of some scales, they are far easier to keep in check and far slower to seriously harm plants.

Moths produce a great number of the caterpillars and worms that chew up fruit and leaves. Few adult moths harm plants, so they're not always connected with the dire results of their having passed through. Among the commonest larvae of moths are cabbage loopers, corn earworms, tent caterpillars, and tomato hornworms.

Among the hard-shelled winged insects called "beetles" are several valuable allies—and some of the most damaging of garden pests. Treasure your ladybird beetles, calasoma beetles, and other ground beetles (see pages 49–50), but be wary of the others in both adult and larval forms. Among the least welcome in this family are asparagus beetles, Colorado potato beetles, Japanese beetles, and Mexican bean beetles. As their names suggest, many beetles favor feeding on a single plant or at most a few related plants. This makes them somewhat easier to manage than some of the general pests and also somewhat easier to identify than they might otherwise be.

The list does not stop here. Mites, nematodes, thrips, and more all make sure gardeners spend plenty of time on the defensive. The following scouting reports will help identify most pest-caused problems—but first, a few simple definitions to help explain the entries:

- Adults are the mature form of insects.
- Grubs are legless young, or larval forms. They burrow in the soil or in fruit.
- Caterpillars are larvae with legs. Some stay in the soil, but most crawl on the surfaces of plants.
- Nymphs are young, resembling adults but smaller. Many are still wingless, while adults are winged.
- Pupae are a transitional form between larvae and adults. Many are protected by shells. They do not feed. Chrysalises and cocoons serve similar purposes.

APHIDS

Black, green, or golden in color, soft-bodied, no bigger than a BB, slower than a snail, and utterly defenseless against a whole host of predators, aphids still prosper because they reproduce so often and in such abundance. Fortunately, they are not especially destructive unless colonies are left to expand unchecked.

Target: any soft tissue, including the new growth of most woody plants

Damage: Juices are sucked from new, tender growth, resulting in wilting or malformation. Some aphids transmit viral diseases.

Life cycle: The young are born live in overlapping generations in mild climates; a winged form deposits eggs in autumn in colder northern states.

Control: pinching, strong jets of water from a hose, adults and larvae of ladybird beetles, larvae of green lacewings, syrphid flies, praying mantises, soap sprays, summer oils

Notes: Adults cluster toward the tips of stems; they are often tended by ants, which gather the honeydew they excrete. Controlling the ants often controls aphids (*see also* mealybugs, scale insects).

ARMYWORMS

Armyworms include several caterpillars of various colors, all between 1 and 2 inches long and likely to feed on leafy vegetables. Beet armyworms are gray-green. Yellow-striped armyworms are purplish to black, with two distinct lengthwise yellow stripes on their backs. Fall armyworms are shiny and brownish, with prominent black spots and a white Y on a black head.

Target: (beet and yellow-striped armyworms) lettuce, spinach, beets, cole crops; (fall armyworm) corn

Damage: Leaves on leafy vegetables are chewed; tips of corn leaves look ragged as they emerge from the center of the stalk.

Life cycle: All armyworms are the larvae of dark-colored, night-flying moths.

Control: hand harvesting, *Bacillus thuringiensis*

Notes: Armyworms favor seedlings, often destroying whole plants.

ASPARAGUS BEETLES

Blue-black mottled with yellow, the asparagus beetle feeds mostly on the plant that gives it its name.

Target: asparagus

Damage: Adults feed on spears and damage them by laying eggs. Adults and gray larvae also feed on fronds.

Life cycle: Overwinters as an adult in early spring to lay bright orange eggs on asparagus spears. Caterpillars hatch quickly.

Control: parasitic wasps, rotenone

Notes: The predatory wasps are common only where there are extensive plantings of asparagus. They both feed on and parasitize asparagus beetle eggs.

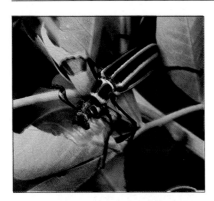

BLISTER BEETLES

Markings of the several species vary greatly, but blister beetles are easily distinguished by chests noticeably smaller than either their heads or abdomens. Most are well under l inch long.

Target: potatoes, tomatoes, peppers, eggplants, sometimes other vegetables

Damage: Adults feed on leaves, causing substantial damage when large populations arrive suddenly.

Life cycle: The larval form hatches in the ground without feeding on foliage.

Control: hand picking, covering with cages, predatory nematodes, sabadilla

Notes: Larvae do not eat foliage; those of some species feed on grasshopper eggs.

CABBAGE LOOPERS

If Groucho Marx had studied cabbage loopers he would have worked them into one of his "walk this way" sketches, but the comedy ends with the gait of this inch-long pale green caterpillar.

Target: broccoli, cabbage, cauliflower, lettuce, spinach, mustard

Damage: Leaves show chewed holes.

Life cycle: The adult form is a gray-brown moth with a silvery spot on each wing. It lays eggs on the undersides of host plant leaves in spring; these hatch into the worm. The last (and most damaging) of three or four generations overwinters as a pupa in a flimsy cocoon attached to a host plant.

Control: hand harvesting, *Bacillus thuringiensis*, rotenone

Notes: Larvae are highly susceptible to *BT* at emergence.

CABBAGE MAGGOTS

The maggot of a small, gray-green fly resembling a housefly is one of the most damaging of the root maggots. Onion maggots are similarly controlled.

Target: cabbage, radishes, rutabagas, turnips

Damage: White, legless maggots burrow in the root, spreading the bacterium of a rot as they feed.

Life cycle: Overwinters as a pupa l to 5 inches underground. The adult fly emerges in spring to lay tiny white eggs at the base of host plants. The eggs hatch into maggots, which then feed on underground parts of the plant.

Control: cheesecloth tents over seed rows (24 threads per inch, spread at least 6 inches on either side of seeds)

Notes: Tents should lift easily for rows to be worked and should stand tall enough for plants to grow unhampered.

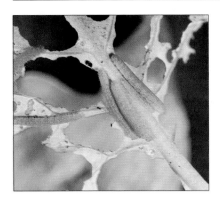

CABBAGEWORMS

Cabbageworms are soft green caterpillars about the size of cabbage loopers but more conventional in gait and further differentiated from them by faint stripes.

Target: broccoli, cabbage, cauliflower

Damage: Leaves show chewed holes.

Life cycle: The adult form is a white butterfly with small black spots on its wings. It lays small yellow eggs on cole leaves. There are four to five generations of caterpillars per year. The cabbageworm overwinters as a chrysalis.

Control: hand harvesting, *Bacillus thuringiensis*, rotenone

Notes: Larvae are highly susceptible to *BT* at emergence.

CODLING MOTHS

Also called "apple worm" and one of the most intractable pests of apples, pears, and other pome fruits, the codling moth is one of the most difficult to deal with organically. The larva is white or pinkish with a shiny black head. Another moth produces a similar but larger and greener larva—called the green fruitworm—that also attacks pome fruit.

Target: apple, pear, English walnut, quince, crabapple, hawthorn trees

Damage: Tunnels may show in immature fruit, usually near the stem or in the dimple at the bottom but also where two fruits touch to give the worm a leverage point.

Life cycle: Overwinters as a mature larva within a cocoon under the bark or in garden debris near the tree. The first moths hatch in May and lay eggs on leaves during bloom. Three generations of larva and moths emerge per year—the larval forms usually in mid-June, late June, and early August. The green fruitworm comes of a moth that overwinters in the soil as an adult or pupa. Fruitworms arrive in June.

Control: hand harvesting, *Bacillus thuringiensis*, ryania

Notes: Flowering quince and apple are prime hosts. Minimizing garden debris near pome fruit trees is one of the best defenses. Dwarfed trees are easier to monitor for cocoons. Tilling the soil may uncover the moth or pupa of the green fruitworm.

COLORADO POTATO BEETLES

The showy polka-dot vest and striped pants are dead giveaways of these smallish beetles, which have spread from their native haunts on the east slopes of the Rocky Mountains to most of the West.

Target: potatoes, tomatoes, eggplants (but can survive on cabbage and weeds)

Damage: Adults and larvae both feed on foliage; the more damaging larvae can completely devour plants if a population is large enough.

Life cycle: Produces two generations per year, with adults of the second overwintering 3 to 6 inches in the soil. This generation emerges in spring; females lay 300 to 500 elongate orange eggs in clusters of 10 or more on the undersides of host plant leaves and then die. The eggs hatch in about a week, quickly developing into larvae.

Control: rotenone

Notes: The larval form has articulated legs and rows of dark spots along both sides. Rotenone is most effective in early May, when the first adults appear on foliage.

CORN EARWORMS

A large green, brownish, or reddish caterpillar closely related to the cutworm is dismaying to find in an ear of corn. But in fact corn earworms do only modest harm; damaged ears can be salvaged by cutting off the spoiled tip.

Target: corn, tomatoes

Damage: Worms and eggs appear in silk and tip kernels of ripening corn; tunnels may show in tomatoes.

Life cycle: In its adult form it's one of the night-flying moths. It overwinters in soil as a shiny brown pupa, emerging in spring to lay eggs in corn silks following each full moon. Caterpillars hatch quickly thereafter.

Control: hand picking, *Bacillus thuringiensis,* summer oil sprayed on forming silks, delayed planting until after egg-laying season

Notes: Corn earworms are easiest to control by balking the moth with an injection of summer oil (or even vegetable oil) into the tips of the corn ears when the silks emerge. Otherwise, catch them early after emergence with *BT.* Tilling disturbs and may kill the pupal form. A very similar caterpillar feeds on geraniums; the most effective control is picking and crushing any buds that show obvious signs of damage before the feeding worm emerges.

CUCUMBER BEETLES

There are three common forms of cucumber beetles, all as small as a ladybird beetle or smaller. The striped cucumber beetle is greenish yellow with three stripes along its back. The western spotted cucumber beetle is orange-yellow, with three rows of black spots. The third form, the banded cucumber beetle, is greenish yellow with three well-defined green bands across its back. Larvae are slim and white.

Target: cucumbers, melons, squashes

Damage: Larvae feed on roots and the underground stem; adults chew on all aboveground portions of a plant.

Life cycle: There are two generations per year. Adults lay eggs around stems of host plants. Adults of the second generation overwinter in soil.

Control: hand picking, predatory nematodes

Notes: Overwintering adults attack seedlings. The spotted form usually damages only young plants. This insect carries the organism of cucurbit wilt.

CURCULIOS

Curculios are beetles resembling other weevils in having a long, curved snout. Most of the several species are host-specific. The plum curculio (shown) is about the size of a ladybird beetle, and one of the hardest pests to control organically in home orchards.

Target: (plum curculio) pome and stone fruits; roses

Damage: The plum curculio cuts the skin of fruit and deposits eggs that become tunneling larvae.

Life cycle: Overwinters as an adult that deposits eggs in forming fruit. After feeding, larvae pupate in the soil. Summer-generation adults emerge in July and feed on fruit until it is time to overwinter.

Control: tilling, nematodes for larvae; hand picking for adults

Notes: Infested fruit ripens before normal fruit; picking and destroying it will diminish the population somewhat.

CUTWORMS

So named because they cut sprouting seedlings off at ground level, cutworms are the night-feeding larval forms of a considerable number of night-flying moths.

Target: many plants, especially newly sprouted seedlings and transplanted tomatoes or cabbage

Damage: Newly sprouted plants disappear overnight; ragged edges and chewed holes are evidence in leaves of older plants.

Life cycle: Adult moths fly only in spring and summer, the larvae are present in several generations throughout the year.

Control: protective collar around base of transplants, hand harvesting, *Bacillus thuringiensis*

Notes: Cutworms feed at night; during daylight they bury themselves curled in a "C" in loose soil or hide beneath boards or other cover on the ground near a food source.

EARWIGS

Mean-looking pincers at earwigs' tails can draw a drop of blood from your fingers, but only if you're uncommonly careless. Still, the weapon makes a fine visual symbol of the menace these ancient insects bring to a garden.

Target: all plants, but especially beans, potatoes, beets, cabbage, cauliflower, peas, dahlias, zinnias, sweet William, figs

Damage: Young leaves, tip growth, petals, and stamens of flowers are chewed. Will tunnel into ripe apples, apricots, cherries, peaches, and plums.

Life cycle: Females lay clusters of 20 to 50 pearly eggs in fall and spring in the upper 2 to 3 inches of soil. Females and some males overwinter as adults.

Control: hand harvesting

Notes: Mainly nocturnal, earwigs seek cool, dark, damp retreats in daylight hours. Look under garden debris and between soil and boards inside raised beds for nests. A loosely rolled newspaper is the perfect trap in which to squash them in numbers. Earwigs generally forage on decaying plant material; keeping the garden clean helps in their control.

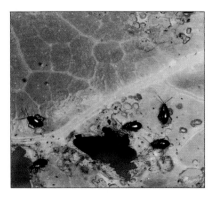

FLEA BEETLES

Flea beetles are small, oval jumping beetles. Most are shiny bronze or dark blue, but one is pale brown with yellowish stripes and another, common to deserts, is black with yellowish legs and antennae. All have an appetite for a broad range of edible plants except for the desert variety, which is partial to corn.

Target: beets, chard, peppers, eggplants, potatoes, radishes, tomatoes, corn

Damage: Adults chew round, irregular "shot holes" in leaves; they seldom seriously threaten the health of vigorous, established plants. Slender white larvae do more damage by chewing on roots; potato tubers may become pimply or silvery from burrows just under the skin or may show superficial tracks.

Life cycle: Adults overwinter in protective weeds. In late spring they lay tiny eggs on the soil around host plants. Larvae feed mostly underground. There are two generations a year.

Control: rotenone

Notes: The most serious threat is to seedlings; healthy older plants survive well. Apply rotenone whenever beetles or leaf damage begin to appear, usually in late May. Keeping weeds down eliminates several favored host plants and holds populations in check to some extent.

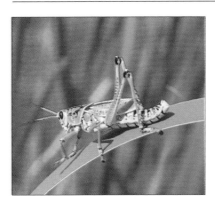

GRASSHOPPERS

Grasshoppers are sort of like tourists: they're not bad one at a time but are unbearable in crowds. Fortunately, they rarely show up in hordes. There are dozens of species differing in size, color, and markings. Some of their relatives are known as cicadas and locusts.

Target: all plants

Damage: Damage is slight from individuals (except to young plants), but hordes will eat plants to the ground.

Life cycle: Overwinters mainly as an egg; nymphs hatch early in spring.

Control: tents over small plants, hand harvesting

Notes: Grasshoppers are slowest and easiest to pick by hand when it is quite cool. The most successful general control is to catch them at their (typically remote) breeding grounds before they start to move. No conventional organic controls have much effect on large populations, though birds tend to attack them; ask anybody in Utah.

HARLEQUIN BUGS

A pest mostly in the south, the ladybird beetle-sized harlequin is one of the true bugs. Varied but always complex, often handsome black-and-orange patterns mark it.

Target: broccoli, cabbage, horseradish, kale, turnips

Damage: Nymphs suck the sap from leaves, which show yellowed patches and then wither. Heavy concentrations can kill plants quickly.

Life cycle: Overwinters as an adult. Eggs laid on the undersides of leaves hatch nymphs beginning in early spring.

Control: hand harvesting, sabadilla, rotenone, pyrethrum

Notes: Hand picking when adults first appear in spring is the best control. Keeping the garden free of spent and decaying plants throughout the growing season helps limit populations. A sabadilla-rotenone-pyrethrum spray works fairly well on nymphs, hardly at all on adults.

JAPANESE BEETLES

Japanese beetles feed on almost everything but the common vegetables.

Target: leaves, blossoms, and fruits of more than 275 species

Damage: Adults can defoliate shrubs; grubs feed heavily on roots, especially of lawns.

Life cycle: Grubs feed in soil for 10 months and then pupate early in spring. Beetles hatch in May or June; the females lay eggs of a new generation in soil through July and August.

Control: parasite wasps, milky spore disease

Notes: Milky spore disease has substantially caught up with the beetle and keeps it in check most of the time.

JUNE BEETLES

Their alternative names—may beetles, june bugs—suggest the june beetles' season in the sun, but it is the earlier soft, white larval form that should worry gardeners. (Incidentally, the similar green june beetle or fig beetle is more common, and neither it nor its larvae harm garden vegetables, feeding instead on decaying matter.)

Target: beans, beets, coles, potatoes, sweet corn, tomatoes

Damage: Grubs can feed heavily on roots; adults may feed on foliage but seldom to a damaging extent.

Life cycle: Larvae overwinter in soil for 2 years then pupate during the third winter. Adults appear every third year.

Control: tilling, nematodes and milky spore disease for larvae; hand picking for adults

Notes: The several species vary widely in color and size (from a half-inch to more than an inch); most buzz; all are attracted to lights.

MEALYBUGS

In the same family as aphids and scales, mealybugs might be described as hard aphids or soft scales. They and woolly aphids are near enough to being twins to treat the same way.

Target: any soft tissue of most plants

Damage: New tip growth is eaten as it emerges; raggedy holes appear in young leaves near tips of branches.

Life cycle: Mealybugs' cycle is the same as aphids'.

Control: hand harvesting, adults and larvae of ladybird beetles, praying mantises, soap solution, summer oils

Notes: Frequently, colonies are dense enough to make a cottony mound on leaves or, oftener, stems.

MEXICAN BEAN BEETLES

People who give human qualities to insects think of these as ladybird beetles who went wrong. What distinguishes them from ladybugs is a greenish yellow to almost bronze hue plus eight black spots on each wing cover. The larvae are yellow with six rows of long, black-tipped spines along their backs. The eastern United States hosts the bean leaf beetle, which is longer and buff colored, with three or four pairs of dark spots and narrow dark borders on its wing covers.

Target: bush, Lima, and pinto beans

Damage: Mexican bean beetle adults and larvae skeletonize leaves by feeding on their undersides; heavy infestations feed on pods and stems as well. Unchecked, they will kill plants. Bean leaf beetles feed on the undersides of leaves and may also chew off seedlings at or just below ground level.

Life cycle: These beetles overwinter in woodlands as adults. The females lay eggs on the undersides of bean leaves in spring; larvae hatch soon after. A second generation of adults hatches from pupae attached to host plants, usually under leaves.

Control: hand harvesting, rotenone

Notes: Sprays must soak undersides of leaves to be effective.

NEMATODES

Nematodes are a large family of worms too tiny to be seen by the naked eye but in the aggregate able to slowly kill plants by feeding on their roots.

Target: all plants (though many species are attracted to single families)

Damage: Most produce root nodules (shown) that inhibit the uptake of nutrients.

Life cycle: Their cycle is essentially continuous.

Control: interplanting some species of marigolds, planting resistant strains of tomato

Notes: Increasingly, nematologists are identifying beneficial species that prey on larval beetles and other soilborne pests. See roster of resources on page 36.

ROSE CHAFERS

The rose chafer is only one among several beetles attracted to roses. It is also—unlike most insects named after a particular plant—a general pest.

Target: roses, many other flowers, some fruits and vegetables

Damage: Adults feed on flowers and foliage; larvae feed on roots (especially of grass) when not hibernating.

Life cycle: Overwinter deep in soil as larvae; emerge in spring for a short feeding period as adults.

Control: net cages over low-growing plants; hand picking for adults; tilling, milky spore disease, and predator nematodes for larvae

Notes: Like most beetles, rose chafers are not easily controlled by organic means. They are poor fliers. Mostly found in or near fallow fields.

SCALE INSECTS

In effect making up the armored division of the aphid army, scales—or cocci—come in several forms. San Jose and Leucanium are two of the more common sorts. Like aphids they are tended by ants.

Target: all plants

Damage: They suck juices from plants wherever they attach, usually on stems or small branches of plants, including woody ones.

Life cycle: Eggs hatch under cover of an adult and then crawl out to their own feeding site during spring or summer.

Control: hand harvesting (scrubbing off with a plastic scouring pad), dormant oil spray

Notes: All forms of scale are born soft and mobile; as their shells harden they fix themselves in place and feed through hollow tubes inserted into the stem of the plant. Thus they are much easier to control when young. Scales are strongly colonial, though individuals may be quite scattered early on in an infestation. Heavy populations can kill branches, sometimes whole plants. Honeydew drip encourages the growth of sooty mold.

SLUGS AND SNAILS

Do they really need further introduction?

Target: all plants

Damage: Leaves and other soft tissues are chewed, seedlings absolutely demolished.

Life cycle: Molluscs may overwinter as eggs but are normally encountered as adults.

Control: hand harvesting, ground beetles, garter snakes

Notes: See special feature on pages 66–67.

SPIDER MITES

Mites are not insects but are closely related to them. They are too small to be seen clearly by the naked eye but cluster so densely that they make up little patches of red, green, or yellow. Some are predators of others, but most suck the juices from plants.

Target: all plants, but especially deciduous fruit trees and conifers

Damage: When mites suck juices from leaves, those leaves may die; needles on entire branches of conifers will die in severe infestations.

Life cycle: Many overwinter as eggs on host trees, but some species overwinter as adults. There are several generations per year.

Control: (in dormant season) dormant oil as late as possible; (in foliage season) soap spray, strong jets of water from hose, lacewing larvae, commercial or natural predator mites, summer oils, sulfur

Notes: To test for suspected infestation, hold white paper under a leaf and rap the stem sharply; if mites are present they will tumble onto the paper and move about on it. Silvery webbing on affected leaves is also a specific symptom of several species. Repeating sprays 7 to 10 days apart may be necessary if your choice is soap, summer oil, or sulfur.

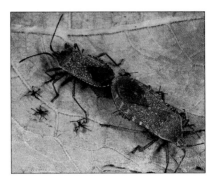

SQUASH BUGS

Members of the group of true bugs, squash bugs feed only on plants of the same name. Adults are about half an inch long. Left unchecked, they will kill a host plant.

Target: squashes, especially winter squashes

Damage: Both adults and nymphs chew on leaves and especially on stems.

Life cycle: Overwinter as adults. In spring, females lay clusters of hard brown eggs on the undersides of squash leaves that hatch as nymphs.

Control: hand harvesting

Notes: Collect and destroy eggs on undersides of leaves. Put out boards or pieces of burlap to trap nymphs and adults; collect and destroy them each morning. Squash bugs may give off an unpleasant odor when crushed.

TARNISHED PLANT BUGS

One of the family of lygus bugs, the tarnished plant bug owes its name to its own mottled brown coloring.

Target: peaches, pears, strawberries, most vegetables

Damage: These bugs gnaw into flower or fruit stems, especially at bud stage, leaving blackened pits. They also blacken terminal shoots.

Life cycle: Overwinter as adults or nymphs in garden debris; there are three to five generations per year.

Control: sticky traps for minor outbreaks; pyrethrum, sabadilla for increasingly serious infestations

Notes: Tarnished plant bugs are not only pests but a carrier for fireblight. Only a quarter-inch long and very agile, they're hard to catch. Keeping the ground clear of debris diminishes breeding spots.

SLUGS & SNAILS

Slugs and snails, the endless battle.

The human race has probably expended more time and energy trying to do away with slugs and snails than it has exploring space. So many have been battling these garden molluscs for so long that there can be no question of the tenacity of these universal garden pests.

Every few years the editors of *Sunset Magazine* poll its readers for new ideas on how to hold back these invaders. The accumulated wisdom is impressive—but barely enough to earn a draw against the oozy enemy.

The most common effective means is hand picking. Successful proponents of this method say the best times to employ it are after 10 P.M. and just before dawn. Both slugs and snails prefer dark, dampness, and temperatures just above the 50°F mark for their moving and feeding. The post–10 P.M. people say watering lightly 2 or 3 hours ahead of time helps lure the enemy into the open.

Snails are easy: just pick them up by the hard, dry shell. Slugs are harder to handle—physically and emotionally—not only because they are slimy all over but because the slime does not wash off with soap and water. Wearing gloves is the first defense. (Rub slime off hands or gloves with salt or use rubbing alcohol, say the veterans.)

The key to the battle is persistence. Daily persistence. Even after the interior of the garden is pretty well under control, the perimeter will forever need watching.

Dispatching the prisoners properly is important to success. The worst thing to do, say old campaigners, is to stomp them and leave the carcasses behind. As often as not eggs in the newly deceased will hatch to produce more snails or slugs.

One recommended solution is to put captives in bags with salt, to be dropped into the garbage. The pitiless stomp them and *then* put their remains in bags for the garbage.

French-trained eaters can make away with European brown snails at dinner (after purging them, please).

Some cannot bring themselves to handle the creatures at all. They can follow the advice of one original thinker who uses a squirt bottle filled half with water, half with household ammonia. Slugs reportedly curl up and die after one squirt. So do snails if you can catch them with their heads outside the shell. The ammonia does nothing to the soil except add a little nitrogen, but it will damage plants if sprayed directly onto leaves.

Copper barriers will actually keep slugs and snails away from prized plants. It seems that slime and copper together produce either a chemical reaction or a slight electrical charge. Either way, both molluscs refuse to cross copper barriers. Copper screening 6 inches high works very well, but disintegrates in about 18 months. Copper sleeves, developed for citrus groves, last for several years and are more cost effective. They come in lengths of 20 feet and can be attached to trunks of individual trees or the outsides of raised beds. There cannot be any gaps nor any drooping branches to serve as bridges.

TENT CATERPILLARS

Wrinkly-hided, blue-striped tent caterpillars are easy to identify in the open and even easier when in their gauzy nests.

Target: fruit trees, especially pome fruit trees

Damage: Leaves are chewed.

Life cycle: The adult form is one of the gray moths that lays eggs on a host plant; the caterpillars hatch in early spring.

Control: pruning away and destroying tents when they first form, *Bacillus thuringiensis*

Notes: The fall webworm produces similar tents but is a different caterpillar, yellow-brown with black-and-orange bumps and tufts of whitish hair. It feeds entirely within its nest, steadily enlarging the web to reach more food. Control it in the same way as the tent caterpillar.

Most other barriers have failed, although a new, salt-impregnated plastic one shows promise.

Country dwellers have reported success using flocks of ducks, with some reservations. The trouble is the ducks. Some people like ducks, but they are not for everyone. Ducks, reported one gardener, absolutely did away with her snails, but were too noisy and dirty to keep around. And geese are just large ducks when it comes to snail patrol.

Good plant selection and garden maintenance will not get rid of these pests, but it can help keep their numbers under control so that picking is less onerous. Try the following:

■ Get rid of old boards, pots, and other hiding places—or else turn them into regularly checked traps. Slipping two plastic 1-gallon nursery cans together creates a dark space between the bottoms of the two cans; lay them on their sides with one or more drain holes close to the ground. Your quarry will crawl through the drain holes during the night and can be disposed of each morning.

■ Clear out plant debris, prune open trees and shrubs, and otherwise help the sun make the ground too dry and warm for the enemy's liking.

■ Do not water plants in the evening, for the same reason.

■ Cultivate the top 4 inches of soil when practicable, destroying any of the pearly, peppercorn-sized eggs you find.

■ Cut back on, get rid of, or plan to use as lures the plants in which slugs and snails most love to hide: agapanthus, amaryllis, artichokes, cannas, daylilies, gazanias, ice plant, irises, ivy, junipers, nasturtiums, primroses, rhubarb, Shasta daisies, star jasmine, and strawberries.

Two durable mollusc myths have lately come in for a good debunking:

■ The idea of salting garden molluscs where they lie has lost favor. For one thing, salt is not good for the soil. For another, too many of the intended victims recover to chomp again.

■ Saucers of beer do well in folklore but less well in practice. Many who have tried it say it only provides slugs with an expensive drink and does not attract snails much, if at all.

THRIPS

Thrips comprise a whole family of small to tiny flies, some of which are fairly general pests, others of which attack only a particular plant. They are a greater problem on ornamentals than edibles.

Target: white and pink rose blossoms, gladiolus leaves and flowers, onions and related plants

Damage: Thrips suck fluids from leaves; in heavy infestations, leaves and flowers will look twisted or will fail to open.

Life cycle: The nymph is wingless, the adult form winged.

Control: adults and larvae of ladybird beetles, lacewing larvae, predatory thrips and mites

Notes: The telltale symptoms of a thrips attack are silvery areas on damaged leaves and wilting. Silvered leaves will not have the webbing characteristic of mite damage.

TOMATO HORNWORMS

Though their size may be daunting, tomato hornworms are slow and obvious and thus easy to control. (Incidentally, their horn is at the back end.) A closely related caterpillar is the tobacco hornworm.

Target: tomatoes, eggplants

Damage: Feeds mostly on leaves but will eat into fruit.

Life cycle: The adult is a large brown moth that flies like a hummingbird. It overwinters in soil as a shiny brown inch-long pupa.

Control: hand picking, *Bacillus thuringiensis*, braconid wasps

Notes: Though hornworms blend into tomato foliage, they leave two distinctive traces: stems stripped bare of leaves and the readily visible black pellets they excrete as they feed. Milk cartons or other shields may keep newly emerged larvae off plants. If you come across a hornworm parasitized by braconid wasps (see page 48), let the wasp eggs finish it off and hatch; you may wish to move the worm to a plant of lesser value. Tilling the soil often turns up pupae of worms that went undetected.

WHITEFLIES

Tiny, waxy, delta-winged sucking insects, the 200-odd species of whiteflies are somewhat damaging on their own. But they're actually double trouble, because the honeydew they secrete encourages a black, sooty mold to form on the leaves of host plants.

Target: almost every garden fruit and vegetable

Damage: The sticky honeydew reduces leaves' ability to photosynthesize; sooty mold often follows.

Life cycle: There are many generations per year of eggs, nymphs, and adults.

Control: (eggs and nymphs) frequent strong hose blasts on both sides of affected leaves; (all forms) soap sprays with complete leaf coverage, ladybird beetles, spiders; (in closed spaces such as greenhouses) Tanglefoot or SAE 90 motor oil on yellow cards

Notes: Absolute control is not needed; all plants can withstand moderate populations. Warm, still air is the perfect environment for whiteflies, so greenhouses are favored spots; one species is even called the "greenhouse whitefly."

WIREWORMS

The shiny brown segmented or jointed larvae of the click beetle, wireworms are the particular bane of gardeners who dote on root crops.

Target: potatoes, carrots, beets, turnips, rutabagas

Damage: Some gnawing on surfaces is obvious, but mainly damage is tunnels into roots and tubers.

Life cycle: Overwinter in soil as adults. Females lay eggs in soil in June; these hatch as larvae within a month, then spend 3 to 5 years in that stage. They are close to the surface during the growing season, deeper in winter.

Control: tilling, nematodes

Notes: Wireworms are most frequently found in wheat country, where they can be extremely destructive in new gardens planted with potatoes for the first time.

DISCOURAGING INSECTS WITH COMPANION PLANTINGS

Many organic gardeners set a great deal of store by pairing two kinds of plants in a bed to discourage insects from attacking not just one but both. At least as many entomologists remain unconvinced.

Using marigolds to discourage pest nematodes is the most often reported success story. These tiny, translucent, soilborne worms can be particularly troublesome to carrots, cole crops, cucumbers, melons, radishes, and tomatoes if allowed to go unchecked in home gardens. Conventional organic pesticides are ineffective against them. However, marigold roots secrete a chemical that kills them on contact. The trick seems to be in getting enough of the poison.

Any variety is supposed to work, but, according to one test, the most effective are French marigolds. 'Tangerine' has performed best. Others are 'Petite Gold,' 'Goldie,' and 'Petite Harmony.'

In tests by the University of Georgia, solid rows of marigolds planted 7 inches apart rid a test plot of nematodes for a year. The flowers were planted in March and April and were removed 4 months later, in time to plant autumn vegetable crops. Similar tests by other nematologists have been less conclusive to outright unsatisfactory.

A simple border planting of marigolds around a vegetable bed does not appear to do much good where nematodes are well established.

Incidentally, marigolds are said not to affect beneficial nematodes, because these do not feed on plant roots. Again, the evidence is sketchy.

Other pairings recommended by organic gardeners have even less evidence from controlled experiments. However, as they can do no harm and might do some good, you may want to try the following:

■ Borage is supposed to discourage tomato worms.

■ Marigolds are thought to be unattractive to whiteflies (and to secrete enough oils onto nearby plants to render them unattractive, too).

■ Spearmint, tansy, and pennyroyal are thought to discourage ants and thus aphids.

Akin to companion planting is "trap planting." The idea here is to lure specific pests to a plant they favor more than one you are trying to keep pest free.

For example, nasturtiums lure aphids away from other susceptible plants, and pots of sprouting grain in greenhouses or next to houseplants can trap gnats.

In trap planting, the key is to monitor the trap plants closely, destroying aphids or other pests as soon as they appear rather than waiting for the populations to build up. (In the case of gnats, boil the sprouted grain and the gnat eggs laid on it every two weeks, putting out a new pot of sprouted grain each time.)

The biggest problem with trap planting is that insects sometimes ignore the cues and go after the plants you treasure rather than the ones they are supposed to favor.

All other aspects of companion planting aside, growing a rich mixture of plants helps minimize pest damage for the simple reason that many pests are host specific. In a garden full of variety, damage by a major pest is seldom widespread.

KEY DISEASES OF GARDEN PLANTS

Fungi and bacteria account for most of the diseases that can be lethal to plants. Viruses add a few more. The following list is limited to a few of the most common plant diseases, especially to ones that attack fruits and vegetables.

As you will discover in reading the entries on individual diseases, keeping a close watch over your garden is the first and most important step in disease control. At the first sign of disease, take steps to get rid of all infected materials. Even before trouble shows up, a steady program of keeping the garden free of debris will lessen the chances of a disease becoming established. Even plant doctors live by the old adage that tells us an ounce of prevention is worth a pound of cure.

FIREBLIGHT

A bacterium, fireblight affects only pomes. It is carried from cankers to blossoms of an infected plant by splashing water or insects and is then transmitted to blossoms of other trees by pollenizing bees.

Target: apple, cotoneaster, crabapple, hawthorn, pear, pyracantha, quince, toyon trees

Damage: Individual leaves and branches wilt and turn soot-black, thus its name.

Control: Prune diseased twigs and burn them as soon as they are cut; disinfect clippers after *each* cut by dipping them in rubbing alcohol for 30 seconds. Make cuts 6 inches below infection on small branches, 12 inches on larger limbs.

LEAF SPOT

Leaf spot—or anthracnose, black spot, scab, or shot hole—is caused by a number of different fungi, hence its several names. The subtribes have further divisions within themselves. Among them, they damage a broad range of plants, especially in regions of high rainfall.

Target: many plants, but in gardens especially strawberries, apples, pears (anthracnose), roses (black spot), apples (scab), and plums and prunes (shot hole)

Damage: Anthracnose causes cankers to appear on limbs or small trunks and irregular brown patches to show up, especially on new leaves; it may cause dieback of tender shoots. Symptoms of black spot are irregular, orange-bordered black spots on leaves and stems. Scab leaves disfiguring lesions on apples and crabapples and, if severe, leads to defoliation. Shot hole results in black spots that sometimes drop out, leaving holes in leaves.

Control: For all, replant with resistant varieties whenever possible. Clean up all fallen leaves and prunings every year, before winter rains if you can. Prune out anthracnose-infected branches whenever symptoms appear and spray with Bordeaux mixture. Spray for apple scab with wettable sulfur or lime-sulfur before flower buds open, again when buds show blossom color, and yet again when three-quarters of the blossom petals have fallen.

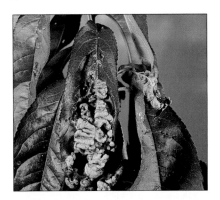

PEACH LEAF CURL

Although this fungus does not do dramatic damage, it slowly weakens infected trees if allowed to go unchecked.

Target: peaches, nectarines

Damage: Midribs of leaves thicken, causing the curl; leaves discolor to pink or red and then drop early.

Control: Spray with fixed copper or lime-sulfur around the first of the year and follow twice at 3- to 4-week intervals (until leaves show). Cover genetic dwarfs with plastic film until leaves show. Pick off and destroy infected leaves (the fungus overwinters in them).

POWDERY MILDEW

In contrast to other fungi, this one flourishes in warm, dry climates rather than moist, cool ones.

Target: beans, peas, squash, dahlias, chrysanthemums, and young growth of many woody plants, including roses and lilacs

Damage: Infects buds, leaves, and stems depending on the strain of mildew and type of host plant. Mainly shows up first as gray or white circular patches on leaves, later as crumpled, distorted, powdery whole leaves.

Control: Avoid planting extremely susceptible varieties of roses and other susceptible plants (such as *Photinia glabra* and *Euonymus japonica*). Spray with lime-sulfur as a dormant spray or lime-sulfur or sulfur when symptoms first appear.

RUST

Most of the fungi called "rust" go after ornamentals. Each is specific to a certain type of plant.

Target: roses, hollyhocks, snapdragons, many others

Damage: Rust usually appears in late spring as yellow-to-orange pustules on the undersides of older leaves, but some rusts are brown, even purple. Eventually shows a mottled yellow on upper surfaces of leaves.

Control: Avoid installing susceptible plants. Clean up fallen leaves and debris during winter; remove any rust-infected leaves that remain on plants. During the growing season, water overhead only in the mornings on sunny days. Control outbreaks with wettable sulfur.

VERTICILLIUM WILT

A widespread fungus, verticillium is a soilborne organism that invades and plugs up the water-conducting tissues in roots and stems. It thrives in cool, moist soil but usually does not reveal its presence until warm, dry weather.

Target: mint, tomatoes, potatoes, cotton, strawberries, certain melons, but also nearly all garden plants, including cherry, maple, and other trees

Damage: One side or one branch of the plant typically wilts. Leaves yellow from their margins inward and then turn brown and die. Wilt progresses from the bottom of the plant upward and from the inner part of branches to the tips.

Control: There is no organic control. Excess nitrogen fertilizer favors the development of wilt. Once soil is infected, install only resistant plants. Crop rotation will not force verticillium to disappear, as it can live in the soil for years with no host plants. Pruning infected limbs from trees can help them recover, as can feeding and watering.

GUIDE TO
PLANTS FOR AN
ORGANIC GARDEN

All through this book, we've hammered at how much a successful organic garden depends on three linked factors: fertile soil, natural pest controls, and intelligent plant selection. Plant selection may be the key of keys. Climate is the major measure. The Arizona desert is no place to grow rhododendrons and Washington's high Cascades are not the spot for saguaro cactus. Nobody needs a book to tell him or her that. Far more mysterious is the fact that some plants prosper or fail within very narrow climate ranges. Most apricots, for example, cannot grow better than they do near Sunset's headquarters at the south end of San Francisco Bay, but no variety of this fruit is likely to survive, let alone prosper, in the Napa Valley, just to the north of that bay. (Hot, dry winds in spring appear to be the culprit; young trees just shrivel up and die when such winds blow.)

However, these are two sorts of extremes. Most of the favored families of plants can be grown almost anywhere you might be if you pay heed to species and variety. By nature apples belong in places like eastern Washington, because most varieties need months of chill winter temperatures to rest up for the burst of energy that produces a full crop of tasty fruit. However, residents of mild-winter climates have liked apples enough to persist until plant breeders could develop a handful of varieties that yield pleasant, if not spectacular, fruit in Los Angeles, where football fans expect to go to the Rose Bowl on New Year's Day in shirt-sleeves. Plant breeders have developed insect- or disease-resistant varieties of many species in the same way. This is not to say that new is always better. Some organic growers have tracked down old, even ancient varieties of fruits, vegetables, and ornamentals that commercial growers have long since abandoned. These old varieties may require too much attention to be profitable on the farm, but they can be enormously satisfying to the home gardener able to lavish extra care in return for incomparable flavors or colors. Species and varietal selection is not a question to be answered from afar. Observe successful gardens in your neighborhood, quiz your county Agri-cultural Extension agent, then push your local nursery to stock what grows best where you are. The rest of the broad rules can be boiled down to these: Choose plants adapted to the kind of soil you have. Group plants by their fertilizer requirements. (Pears, for example, are subject to fireblight if they get much nitrogen, so they should not be sited near plants that need it in large doses.) The same advice holds true for water. Place plants with careful regard for sun and shade, and shelter them from wind, if that's a consideration, too. The following list of plants sticks to a few favorite vegetables, fruits, and ornamentals. Though there is some general information, the emphasis is on organic requirements.

VEGETABLES

ARTICHOKES. The artichoke is a fine ornamental plant as well as a food producer. As a vegetable it grows best where summers are cool and moist: the commercial centers are along California's fog-girt central coast between San Francisco and Monterey. Roots are deep, fleshy, and perennial, requiring richly organic soil with a pH of close to 6.0. The plants must have good drainage; set them in raised beds if hardpan or heavy soil is a problem. Plant dormant roots in winter or early spring; set the root shanks vertically, with growth buds or shoots just above soil level. Plants should be 4 to 6 feet apart.

For vegetable production artichokes must never have their growth checked, which means that roots must always be moist. Water thoroughly once a week, more often in dry heat. Harvest buds when they are plump but still tight.

At the end of the season, cut off the old stalks near the ground in mild-winter areas. Where winters are cold, cut plants down to 12 inches, tie the stubbed stalks over the crown, and mulch heavily.

Artichokes need to be divided and replanted every fifth year. To encourage more of the edible buds, trim off all but the three strongest shoots when plants sprout in spring.

The plant prospers in slightly acidic soil with a high organic content and is a heavy nitrogen feeder. Work coarse-ground bonemeal into the soil at planting and fertilize with nitrogen before new growth starts. Artichokes also profit from a mid-season side-dressing (commercial growers favor chicken manure).

Artichokes are favorites of slugs and snails, which tend to hide deep in the leaves, and of aphids (control with strong jets of water or a soap spray). Earwigs hide in and feed on the buds; if plants are meant for food, control earwigs by trapping them in rolled newspapers placed on the ground near the plants.

ASPARAGUS. The main edible crop ripens from spring through early summer, before the hottest weather arrives. After that the plants can be fairly attractive ornamentals in mild climates. Plant asparagus in fall or winter—or in early spring where winters are cold.

Two weeks before you plan to plant, dig a trench 1 foot wide and deep, long enough to space plants 18 inches apart. Work in 6 inches of manure or compost plus a healthy sprinkling of bonemeal and potash with the soil at the bottom of the trench.

At planting, soak thoroughly before setting topmost roots about 6 inches below the trench lip. Spread out roots evenly and then cover with 2 inches of soil. Water. Leave the remaining soil alongside the trench until the plants begin to grow. As they grow, add soil so that only the tips remain exposed. When the trench is filled, allow the spears to emerge. Do not harvest them for food the first year; instead, allow foliage to help build strong roots. Keep soil constantly moist.

In succeeding years—and strong plants yield for a decade—harvest until spears begin to be thin. At this point, fertilize and allow foliage to grow through the rest of the season. In cold-winter climates, mulch the plantings heavily before frosty nights arrive, leaving the dead stems to catch snow as secondary insulation for the roots.

Asparagus prospers in fertile, well-drained sandy loam or clay loam with a pH of 6.0 to 6.7.

It is a heavy nitrogen feeder. In spring, fertilize with nitrogen, phosphorus, and potash (as fish meal or cottonseed meal); then mulch with compost or well-rotted manure to augment the fertilizer and moderate soil temperatures. Fertilize again when you stop harvesting spears.

Plants are subject to asparagus beetles, which can be controlled with rotenone, and aphids, which can be hosed off.

BEANS. Beans come in a great variety for eating fresh or drying. String beans, Lima beans, soybeans,

fava beans . . . the list goes on.

All save favas are warm-weather crops that will not begin to grow until the ground warms. Sow seeds 1 inch deep and 3 inches apart in rows 2 to 3 feet apart. If they don't sprout, chances are they rotted in too-cool or too-damp soil.

Flood-irrigate plantings regularly (shallow furrows between rows will help). Avoid overhead watering; it encourages mildew. Mulch to conserve moisture and keep soil temperatures even. Production should begin 2 to 3 months after planting.

Beans prosper in any well-drained soil with a pH of 6.0 to 6.8.

They are moderate nitrogen feeders. If you feed beans at all after planting, fertilize with nitrogen only until pods begin to develop; too much nitrogen produces foliage at the expense of a crop. Treating bean seed with an inoculant allows plants to provide their own nitrogen.

Most varieties are subject to Mexican bean beetles, aphids, leafhoppers, and spider mites. Downy mildew is the principal disease.

BEETS. Beets demand cool weather—mild summers are best, spring and autumn acceptable substitutes in warmer areas. Sow seed as soon as the ground can be worked in spring and up to a month thereafter. In mild-winter areas they can be a winter crop, sown in autumn. Maturity is 55 to 80 days from seed.

Beets do best in even-textured, sandy loam, which "gives" enough for the root to form and expand yet has enough organic matter to retain moisture during the growing season. Soil pH should be in the 6.0 to 6.8 range. Work in bonemeal and potash before planting, and mulch to keep soil temperatures even. Overhead watering keeps greens and roots crisp.

Moderate nitrogen feeders, beets will need only a light feeding when plants are 5 to 6 inches high if the soil is well prepared at planting.

The greens are subject to flea beetles and, sometimes, to leaf miners (removing and destroying infested leaves controls them nicely). The fleshy root may be infested by nematodes and wireworms.

BROCCOLI. Defying assorted small children's opinions, broccoli remains a home garden favorite. It matures from seedlings in 60 to 80 days, from seed in 120 to 150. Pick the flower head and about 6 inches of stem from the central stem when the head is still hard and green. Plants will continue to produce for about 2 or 3 months if you keep the lateral heads cut. Hot weather results in poorer-quality heads. To perform best, broccoli needs the same watering program as its close relative, cabbage.

The plants prosper in highly organic soil with a pH of 6.0 to 6.8. They are moderately heavy nitrogen feeders: fertilize every 3 or 4 weeks with blood meal (1 tablespoon to 1 gallon of water) or a liquid fish product.

Broccoli is subject to cabbage loopers, cabbageworms, cabbage maggots, aphids, flea beetles, and harlequin bugs. Its diseases include downy mildew and fusarium wilt.

BRUSSELS SPROUTS. Though they may look like bizarre dwarf palm trees, Brussels sprouts are a cole. Like other coles, they are a cool-season crop. They take about 4 months to mature from seed, so they should be planted early in spring or, in mild-winter climates, in summer for winter harvest. Water them as you would cabbage. Harvest the small heads on the central stem from the bottom up, always before they change color from pale to dark green. Always leave the top leaves on, to manufacture food for the plant. If snows arrive before the last heads ripen, pull up the plant, take it into shelter, pack soil around its roots, and continue harvesting.

Brussels sprouts perform best in highly organic soil with a pH of 5.5 to 6.8.

They are moderately heavy nitrogen feeders: fertilize every 3 or 4 weeks with blood meal (1 tablespoon to 1 gallon of water) or a liquid fish product.

They are prey to cabbage loopers, cabbageworms, cabbage maggots, aphids, flea beetles, and harlequin bugs. Their principal diseases are downy mildew and fusarium wilt.

CABBAGE. Cabbage is the classic cole crop. A cool-season grower, its planting must be timed so that it reaches maturity before or after the hot summer months. If it approaches maturity in hot weather it will bolt: fail to form a head and start producing seed. Early varieties mature in 90 to 125 days, late ones in 125 to 150. In cold-winter areas, set plants out as early as possible in spring. Plant in midsummer for autumn crops (or in the early autumn where summers are hot).

From seed, it takes about 6 weeks for plants to grow enough to be set out. Space them 18 inches apart in a row and make the rows 30 inches apart. Set the young plants in more firmly and deeply than most other vegetables, because they become quite top-heavy. It is vital to keep an even moisture level. If plants dry out, their heads often crack. Because cabbages mature so slowly, you can interplant them with radishes, lettuce, or spinach to gain space. They prosper in highly organic soil with a pH of 6.0 to 6.8 and very good drainage.

Cabbages are moderately heavy nitrogen feeders. Fertilize every 3 or 4 weeks with blood meal (1 tablespoon to 1 gallon of water) or a liquid fish product.

Cabbages are subject to cabbage loopers, cabbageworms, cabbage maggots, aphids, flea beetles, and harlequin bugs. Although *Bacillus thuringiensis* works well against the two leaf-eating caterpillars, covering the plants with netting prevents moths from laying eggs and keeps feeding insects away as well. If you plant for autumn crops you'll avoid their egg-laying season altogether. Cabbages may be infected with downy mildew and fusarium wilt.

CARROTS. Carrots absolutely demand even-textured soil in order not to grow into peculiar shapes. Rocks will surely deform the roots, but even lumps of clay or fibrous elements such as peat moss will send them off in unwanted directions. Gardeners have a full choice when it comes to soil depth. Some varieties are as short as 2 or 3 inches but make up for it with thick diameters. Others grow more than a foot long.

(Continued on next page)

Bush beans mulched with straw

'Earking' corn thriving in summer sun

. . . *Carrots*

Carrots and beets will grow well together in cool climates; carrots withstand heat a bit better. Space rows 12 inches apart. Thin seedlings to 1 inch apart. Later, harvest baby carrots, leaving plants 2 inches apart to grow to full size. Roots mature in 65 to 75 days from sowing. Steady moisture is crucial, especially between sowing and germination.

In addition to being even textured, soil for carrots must be well-drained sand or sandy loam with a pH of 5.5 to 6.8. Building raised beds with specially prepared soil is one way to cope with problem soil.

Carrots are moderate nitrogen feeders. If the soil is enriched with bonemeal and potash before planting, a light feeding of nitrogen when the tops are 6 inches high should provide all the boost the roots will need to get to harvest.

The plants are subject to carrot rust flies, which lay eggs on the soil at the crown of the plants. Their maggots feed on the roots; your best defense is laying netting over the row from sprouting to harvest time. Aphids, leafhoppers, and nematodes are other potential pests.

CAULIFLOWER. Along with broccoli, Brussels sprouts, and cabbage, cauliflower is one of the cole crops, a ready performer in cool climates or a late-season crop in regions with warm summers. In fact, cauliflower tolerates heat even less than cabbage does. Space plants 2½ to 3 feet apart in rows 3 feet apart. Plants are ready to eat about 2 months after they are set out. Because cauliflower matures slowly and is heat sensitive, interplanting with other crops to shade the soil will help. Start lettuce, radishes, or onions with the cauliflower sets. When these plants are taken out they can be replaced by bush beans or peas, which will then ripen along with the cauliflower. To protect forming heads, pull the outer leaves over them and tie them together with string.

Cauliflower prospers in highly organic soil with a pH of 6.0 to 6.8.

A medium to medium-heavy nitrogen feeder, it benefits from a nitrogen dosage every 3 to 4 weeks throughout its growing season.

It is subject to cabbage worms, cabbage loopers, cabbage maggots, aphids, flea beetles, and harlequin bugs. Diseases include downy mildew and verticillium wilt.

CELERY. Celery partakes of the general trend for leafy vegetables to grow well in cool climates. It may even outperform the coles in this regard. The tastiest celery is kept in the dark for 3 to 4 weeks before harvesting. Some people tie the stalks into a tight cluster and mound soil up around them. Others remove both ends from sizeable tin cans (3-pound coffee cans are perfect) and slip them over the head of the plant so stalks will blanch.

Celery grows best in richly organic sandy loam with a pH of 6.0 to 6.8. It is a medium to medium-heavy nitrogen feeder, benefiting from a nitrogen application every 3 to 4 weeks.

Pests include aphids, cabbage loopers, leafhoppers, and nematodes.

CHARD. Chard has much the same kind of leaves as beets do but is a better choice for gardeners faced with long, hot summers. Otherwise, it takes the same conditions as beets, prospering in a wide range of heavy to sandy and only moderately fertile soils with a pH of 6.0 to 6.8.

A medium-low nitrogen feeder, it will get along without feeding during the growing season, though a mild fertilizer will produce finer leaves.

Chard is subject to flea beetles and leaf miners; the latter can be controlled by removing infested leaves.

COLLARDS. The durable popularity of collard greens in the South reflects its ability to handle summer heat. Less predictably, this headless cabbage grows sweeter after it is touched by a light frost. In cold-winter areas most gardeners set out plants in spring and then plant seeds in late summer. Where winters are milder, plants can be set out or seeds sown in both spring and summer.

Collards should be placed 12 to 18 inches apart in rows 2 to 3 feet apart; they will grow to 3 feet tall. The plants need rich soil with a pH in the range of 5.5 to 6.8. The soil can be moderately heavy, for this is a thirsty plant that must be kept moist if the leaves are to stay tender.

It's a medium to medium-heavy nitrogen feeder, benefiting from a nitrogen application every 3 to 4 weeks.

Collards are subject to cabbage-worms, cabbage loopers, cabbage maggots, aphids, and harlequin bugs.

CORN. The grand old tradition of setting the water aboil and then going out to harvest a dinner's worth of ears is not as necessary as it used to be. Several varieties now stay sweet for hours, even days, but the time-honored sprint from corn patch to waiting kettle is still fun—and a delicious idea.

It takes a warm summer to ripen almost any corn, but especially the sweetest kinds. The plants need abundant care as well—boosters of fertilizer when they are 1 foot tall and again when they are a shade over 2 feet (bantam varieties when they are less tall). The soil around corn plants must be moist all the time after silks begin to form, which means frequent deep soakings.

Expect two ears per plant, three if you're lucky. To pollinate properly, corn has to be planted in a square, or at least a rectangle several rows wide. Rows need to be 3 feet apart or a bit less, and plants within a row should be 6 inches apart.

As much as it demands moisture, corn also needs well-drained soil to perform well. The soil pH should be between 5.8 and 6.8.

Corn is a voracious nitrogen feeder throughout its 60- to 100-day growing season. A rich mix of compost or manure dug into the soil at seed-planting time may carry the plants through, but the two supplemental feedings mentioned earlier will guarantee fuller ears. The plants are subject to aphids, armyworms, corn borers, corn earworms, and flea beetles. The fibrous plants are not affected by many diseases.

CUCUMBERS. Cucumbers come in scores of sizes, shapes, and colors: big ones for slicing, smaller ones for pickling. All of them are almost as prolific as zucchinis . . . if you meet their requirements.

For starters, cucumbers must be pollinated. Old standard varieties bear both male and female flowers, but many hybrids put out only female flowers. Seed packets of such hybrids contain some male seeds (usually color-coded); these must be inter-planted with the female plants to get a crop.

The plants sprawl, so they need ample space or a trellis. The usual scheme is to mound hills 4 to 6 feet apart in every direction and plant four to six seeds in each. Each hill is later thinned down to three healthy seedlings. Some bush varieties take less space, handy for smaller gardens.

The plants need considerable water in long, deep soaks, or their fruit will taste bitter. All cucumbers thrive in rich, well-drained soils with a pH of 5.5 to 6.8.

Rich soil at planting provides sufficient nutrition. Cucumbers are susceptible to aphids, cucumber beetles, flea beetles, mites, and squash bugs. Their principal diseases are downy mildew and powdery mildew. To minimize the risk of downy mildew, flood-irrigate rather than watering from overhead.

EGGPLANT. Eggplant got its name when the fruits were typically white and about the size of hens' eggs. Such varieties still exist, but the staple varieties produce large, shiny, purple fruits that look nothing like eggs.

Eggplants are cousins of tomatoes and peppers. Like peppers, they require considerable heat to ripen. Regions with 60 to 90 hot days and warm nights (of 65°F or higher) best meet the needs of eggplants.

As they're a fairly good size, the plants should be spaced 24 to 30 inches apart in rows 3 feet apart. Large-fruit varieties should be thinned to six fruits per plant to ripen well. Eggplants thrive in fertile, well-drained soil with a pH of 5.5 to 6.8. For full yield, keep the soil moist. Well-prepared soil should contain enough nutrients, but you can also fertilize during the growing season. Compost can do double duty as a moisture-saving mulch and a mild fertilizer. Avoid high-nitrogen fertilizers; they produce too much

foliage and not enough fruit.

Eggplant pests include aphids, Colorado potato beetles, flea beetles, whiteflies, and tomato hornworms. The significant disease is verticillium wilt.

GARLIC. The stinking rose, as its admirers call it, is a nearly foolproof plant to grow. Use disease-free sets from a nursery, put them in a sunny spot with rich soil, and they will surely perform.

Set out the bulbs in autumn where winters are mild, in early spring where winters are harsher. They should be set about 1 inch deep, 4 to 8 inches apart, in rows about 15 inches apart. The pointed end goes up.

Keep the bed weeded and the soil moist. Pinch off any blossoms that form. Stop watering as soon as leaf tips turn brown, pressing the leaves flat to the ground to prevent flower-ing and hasten the maturing of the flavorful bulb.

Connoisseurs harvest garlic with a garden fork because pulling them up by the leaves tends to crack the bulbs, decreasing their storage life.

Garlic grows best in rich soil with a pH of between 5.5 and 6.8. Not a heavy feeder, it shouldn't need fertilizing during the growing season.

Only aphids and thrips are common pests; no major diseases afflict garlic.

JICAMA. A Mexican root vegetable, jicama (pronounced HEE-ca-ma) is yet another crop that beginning organic gardeners can expect to grow well with little or no trouble.

But it's not all a piece of cake: the vines grow to 25 feet long and must have space or be trained on a trellis.

As its origins suggest, it needs a long, warm growing season; southern California and southern Florida are the perfect locales. The tubers usually ripen between late August and early October if seeds are planted a month after the last frost, but they can be left in the ground so long as there's no frost. (One frost is enough to start them rotting.) Seeds are poisonous.

Jicama requires well-drained sandy loam with a pH in the neigh-borhood of 6.8. The soil must remain moist. The plants are heavy nitrogen feeders, needing monthly doses of nitrogen.

They are not susceptible to any important pests or diseases.

KALE. Another of the fancier relatives of cabbage, kale can be grown in much the same way, in much the same climates. (Frost sweetens its flavors; summer heat makes it more bitter.)

It thrives in fertile soils with a pH of 5.5 to 6.8.

Kale's principal pests are aphids, cabbage loopers, cabbageworms, cabbage root maggots, and flea beetles. Fusarium wilt is its most common disease.

LEEKS. Occasionally described as fat, slow, mild onions, these treasures of the French kitchen make you wait for them but are not troublesome plants.

They fare best in full sun in cool climates, but may grow well in shady spots where summers are warm.

As they grow, mound soil up around the stalks to blanch them—this keeps the edible stalks white and hence mild in flavor. Mounded soil should not reach above the clearly visible leaf joint, so that grains of earth don't work their way down into the bulbs.

Maturation time, from setting out plants to harvesting edible stalks, is at least 4 but more likely 7 months. In cold-winter, mild-summer areas, set plants out in 5-inch-deep furrows from springtime on. Where summers are hot, start them in autumn. To grow from seed, sow in containers 6 to 8 weeks before you plan to set them out.

Leeks grow best in richly organic soil with a pH of 6.0 to 6.8. Soil should drain well but be kept moist. If the soil was rich at planting, no supplementary feeding should be needed in spite of the long pull to maturity.

Thrips are the major insect pest of leeks.

LETTUCE. American cookery has come a long way since lettuce meant iceberg lettuce, period. Kitchen

gardening has moved right along with it, so that now you have five classes to choose among and scores of varieties within each class.

Your choice is important, not only for flavorful salads but also because all lettuces are rather strictly adapted to narrow climate ranges. This is the vegetable that most repays consultation with your county Agricultural Extension agent or other expert on local growing conditions.

Here's a quick introduction to the classes and varieties:

Leaf lettuce. As its name suggests, leaf lettuce produces loosely clustered leaves rather than a head. This class has the greatest number of varieties and is the easiest to grow. Varietal colors range from red or bronze to dark green to chartreuse. Textures are smooth, puckered, ruffly, even frilly. Some varieties, such as 'Green Ice', are slow to go to seed. 'Slo-bolt' was bred to tolerate more summer heat than most without bolting.

Leaf lettuce's quick maturity—within 40 to 50 days—makes it a favorite where spring swiftly gives way to hot summers.

Butterhead lettuce. This type forms heads, but they are soft, loose ones almost like rose blossoms. It is one of the least heat-tolerant classes. Further, it takes 65 to 80 days to mature.

Kitchen gardeners in warm climates can ignore the climate problems if they are willing to plant early and harvest the leaves early should the weather turn hot. Kitchen gardeners in cool climates often plant the rows overtight so they can thin—and eat—the crop while it is still at its youngest and tenderest. But one of the universal advantages of lettuce is that it is delicious at all stages.

Romaine, the sturdy, stiff-leafed stuff of Caesar salad, is one of the most flavorful of lettuces. It is as sensitive to heat as butterhead and takes even longer to mature: figure on 80 days at a minimum. Some gardeners in hot-summer regions where frosts continue late into spring start their romaine indoors long before the last freezing night.

Crisphead lettuce. Crisphead is a truer name for the firm-headed class most of us call iceberg. 'Iceberg' is, in

Bed planted in lettuces

fact, one of the varieties in this class. As a class, crispheads are somewhat more heat tolerant than the butterheads but still fare best in cool-summer climates. 'Imperial No. 44', 'Premier Great Lakes', 'Minetto', and 'Mirage' are among the most heat-resistant varieties.

Celtuce. This fifth class is celery times lettuce. It is still more novel than commonplace in the garden. The plants look and taste like lettuce when young but turn stalky like celery as they approach maturity. The flavor shifts somewhat along with the change in appearance.

Otherwise celtuce behaves much as lettuce does: faring best in cool climates, tending to bolt in overwarm ones.

All the lettuces grow best in fertile, well-drained soils with a pH in the range of 6.0 to 6.8. Soil must be kept moist but never soggy. Mulching to keep soil temperatures stable can be of some help in warm regions.

Lettuce attracts a long roster of salad-loving leaf chewers other than people: aphids, cabbage loopers, cutworms, flea beetles, leafhoppers, leaf miners, slugs, and snails. Downy mildew and fusarium wilt are its major diseases.

ONIONS. Even people who won't eat onions as such eat a fair amount disguised in one way or another. That fact, combined with the relative ease of growing them, makes these pungently flavored vegetables one of the most common inhabitants of kitchen gardens.

Like all other vegetables, onions come in a wide variety. Only Granexes are commonly known, and they're more likely to be called Maui onions or Walla Walla Sweets, or to have some other geographic moniker indicating that heat and soil come together to produce such sweet bulbs that the anointed will eat them as if they were apples. That sweetness may be too much to aim for in a home garden elsewhere, but it's a reminder that, even in onions, selection by variety does matter.

You can start onions in any of three ways.

Sets are miniature dormant onions raised especially for propagation. They are easy to manage and quick to produce. However, to get full-sized bulbs you must select only the smallest sets available. Larger ones are good only for green onions, because they tend to bolt into flower at first warmth, not giving bulbs time to develop size and flavor.

Sets are best planted in spring in cool-summer regions, in autumn where summers are hot and winters mild.

Transplants are actively growing young onions. Their advantage over sets is that they are less apt to bolt before the bulbs become well fattened. Put them out at about the same time you would sets.

Seeds are the slowest route to onions and the one requiring the most care, especially in the first months. Their chief advantage is a far broader selection of varieties than is available with either sets or transplants. Plant seeds in autumn where summers are hot for winter-into-spring crops.

However they start, all onions require steady attention during their growing season. Beds of young plants need to be kept weed free, because shallow onion roots are weak competitors for nutrients. Soil moisture has to be constant, especially during the first months when the bulbs grow most rapidly. Erratic watering balks full development.

Onions are fairly heavy feeders. Even rich soils may not provide enough food to nourish the scanty root system. Almost all successful growers apply a side-dressing of a balanced fertilizer 40 to 60 days after planting.

They require rich, well-drained, loosely textured soil with a pH of 6.0 to 6.8.

The principal pests of onions are thrips and wireworms. Downy mildew can be a troublesome disease.

PEAS. Peas are not only a great food crop; they are a great rehabilitator of planting beds depleted of nitrogen by a prior crop of heavy feeders such as corn. Their modest nitrogen needs allow the soil to rebuild naturally.

Peas can be divided into English and southern types—and then subdivided again.

English peas include all the ones cooks shell, plus sugar peas (grown for edible pods) and snap peas. The latter include varieties eaten as pods before the peas form, eaten shell and pod together like beans, or held until fully mature for shelling.

Southern peas (actually a kind of vetch) are less finely textured; they count cowpeas, crowder peas, black-eyed peas, and field peas among their tribe. They can be picked green for shelling or left on the vine to dry for long storage.

English and southern peas are not the same plants; hence, their needs are not entirely similar.

English peas are cool-summer vines that require moderately rich to rich soil with a pH of 5.5 to 6.8. "Rich" in this case means a high organic content but little nitrogen. An excess of nitrogen produces excess foliage, few peas. Except for a few bush varieties, they must be trellised for support.

Aphids and cucumber beetles are the primary pests of English peas, powdery mildew their most usual disease.

Southern peas are of African origin. They thrive in sweltering, humid summers that wilt their English cousins. Conversely, the cooler the region, the less likely they are to ripen to a sizeable crop. Early-season dwarf or bush varieties are the best bet.

Southern peas get by in less organically rich soil than do English peas, though their pH requirement is identical. They need even less nitrogen.

Their principal pests include aphids, thrips, and nematodes; they're not seriously bothered by diseases.

PEPPERS. Peppers give heat only when they get heat—but even the sweet ones need a growing season in which the days are consistently warmer than 70°F. The ideal average for hotter types is closer to 85°F. All types grow best where they get a lot of sunshine, not too much humidity, no strong winds, and cool nights. The affinity of hot peppers for this climate is readily apparent in their importance to the cuisine of the desert Southwest and the hotter parts of Mexico.

Among the sweet peppers, bells are the most familiar family. They grow on stiff, compact, large-leafed bushes, maturing in 60 to 80 days. Bells and other sweets can be grown almost anywhere except high atop mountains and in the far northern states. They can be picked green (which makes the plants more productive) or left to ripen to bright yellow or red hues.

Smaller sweet varieties include pimientos, pointed Italian frying peppers, sweet Hungarian peppers, and cherry peppers. These are more intensely flavorful than bells but just as sweet. To be at their best pimientos should be harvested only after they are fully red; the others can be harvested at any color stage.

Hot peppers grow on taller, more spreading plants than do sweet ones, and they ripen later under the same growing conditions. Some hot varieties will grow in northern climes, but they fail to become as hot. Some peppers' names tell you they're going to be hot—Tabasco, for example. Some are simply known to be hot varieties: jalapeños and pasillas are among them. Others are just a touch sneaky about it. Hungarian Wax Hots look like Sweet Hungarians, and Hot Cherry Peppers resemble their sweet counterparts. Inspect the labels closely when you buy. Except for jalapeños, which should be harvested when they are dark green, hot peppers are best harvested after they have turned yellow or red.

Sun and heat aside, all peppers require about the same growing conditions. They prosper best in fertile, well-drained soil within a pH range of 5.5 to 6.8. If the soil has been prepared well, peppers will need no further feeding during their growing season. Keep the soil moist but not soggy, especially during flowering and fruiting. Keep weeds and other competition for moisture out of the bed. If a really hot spell shuts the plants down, let them stay in the garden. When the weather cools down, they usually resume fruiting.

Space peppers 18 to 24 inches apart in rows 30 to 36 inches apart.

The plants are subject to—but are not notorious prey of—aphids, armyworms, Colorado potato beetles, corn borers, and mites.

POTATOES. Potatoes and tomatoes are relatives, though you have to wonder how they got that way. Tomatoes grow fat, juicy, sugary fruit above ground; potatoes grow bulbous, starchy tubers deep in the soil.

You would think tomatoes would be the sunny-tempered members of the family, but not so. Whereas tomatoes are a notoriously uncertain crop, potatoes are reliably rewarding, easy-to-grow producers.

Potato varieties are distinguished by size, skin color, and ripening time, but varieties are less important than is the case for most other edible crops. All potatoes are cool-climate plants.

Plant only certified (disease-free) seed potatoes bought from a nursery. Planting potatoes bought from a store as food is unlikely to produce a satisfactory crop, because they've usually been treated to inhibit the growth of eyes. Just prior to planting, cut seed potatoes into chunks about 1½ inches square, each square containing at least two eyes. Plant these in furrows 4 inches deep and 12 to 18 inches apart in rows 30 to 36 inches apart. Cover the chunks with 2 inches of soil after planting; add another 2 inches when they sprout.

At planting time fertilize in bands along each side of the row with a mild, complete fertilizer. (Too much nitrogen produces excess foliage at the expense of tubers.) A light layer of manure the length of each row will be enough if some manure or compost was dug into the soil before planting.

While the plants grow, keep soil uniformly moist and continue to mound it up around the tubers' base to protect them from sunburn and to ensure that no part of them remains green in color. (Green potato flesh is mildly poisonous. If you see any after harvesting, cut it off before cooking.)

"New" potatoes are ready to harvest when the plants flower, 90 to 120 days from planting. Mature varieties are ready when the foliage turns yellow or brown. The latter can be stored if they are not damaged during harvest and if you let them harden for 10 to 15 days after cutting off the vines and ceasing to irrigate. (Use a spading fork, keeping the tool 8 to 16 inches from the plant and lifting gently to minimize punctures.)

Potatoes require fertile but sandy soil that's fast draining and quite acidic. Their preferred pH range is from 4.8 to 5.4. Plants will grow in soils with a pH higher than 5.4, but they become increasingly prone to scab when they do.

Potato plants are subject to aphids, Colorado potato beetles, flea beetles, and leafhoppers. The tubers themselves may be attacked by wireworms. Potatoes are also subject to several viruses, but mainly in commercial plantings . . . home gardeners seldom have to worry about these diseases.

SPINACH. Although it first grew in Iran, true spinach was and is strictly a cool-weather crop.

What limits spinach to cool-weather regions is its habit of suddenly bolting to flower when warm weather strikes. Once it bolts, it's a loss as a food crop. Gardeners in warm-summer regions can grow it in early spring or late autumn. Those with no hope at all can substitute taste-alike New Zealand spinach, Malabar spinach, or tampala—none of these is a true spinach, but all make good salad or cooking greens.

To harvest a spring crop, you should sow spinach seeds 6 to 8 weeks before the last frost date. For an autumn crop, sow seeds 4 to 6 weeks before the first frost date. In mild-winter areas, sow seeds during the winter. To get a summer crop of New Zealand spinach, sow seeds at least 1 week after the last frost or when the soil temperature warms up to 60°F. For an autumn crop, sow seeds at least 8 weeks before the first frost date. Sow Malabar spinach seeds in early summer to midsummer.

Plant seeds a half-inch deep and 1 inch apart in rows 12 to 30 inches apart; later, thin the seedlings to 3 to 4 inches apart. Space New Zealand spinach rows 36 to 60 inches apart and thin seedlings to 12 to 18 inches apart. Vinelike Malabar plants need to be 1 foot apart after thinning and will need supports. Rows should be 18 to 30 inches apart.

The plants of all these leafy vegetables perform best in well-drained, fertile soil having a pH of 6.0 to 6.8.

True spinach is subject to aphids, cabbageworms, and leaf miners. Nematodes are a problem for New Zealand spinach. Malabar attracts no major pests.

SQUASH & PUMPKIN. Organic gardens almost everywhere yield rewarding crops of squashes with only a modest effort. The vast tribe divides itself into two main groups: summer squash and winter squash. Summer squashes are planted for warm-weather harvest and are eaten—skin, immature seeds, and all—while the fruit is small and tender. Winter squashes mature more slowly and become somewhat to a whole lot bigger. Harvest time is in late summer, when the flesh has grown hard and the seeds are mature. They are called "winter" squash because their hard shells allow them to be stored through the cold months.

Among the old-time summer squashes are zucchini, scallop, crookneck, and straightneck. Hybridizers have played scores of variations on these themes—zucchini alone comes in an endless variety of shapes, sizes, and colors.

Prime winter squashes are acorn, banana, butternut, Hubbard, and, to be sure, pumpkin. Quite a few specialty and/or novelty squashes also number among this lot. Spaghetti squash looks like an overgrown zucchini from the outside, but once it's cooked its flesh falls into spaghettilike strands. Melon squash has sweeter flesh than other squashes, though it tastes more like yam than like any melon. It does live up to its name by growing in almost exactly the same warm-to-hot conditions as do watermelons.

Many veteran gardeners plant squash between a shallow irrigation channel and a parallel low mound; the vines are arranged so as to grow along the mound, allowing the roots to be flood-irrigated without wetting the soil beneath the growing fruit. In this system seeds should be sown 2 to 3 inches deep and 12 to 18 inches apart. Thin to 3 to 8 feet apart, depending on the vigor of the vines. A good many long-time gardeners still plant their squash in hills, four or five seeds to a hill then thinned to the best two young vines per hill. The hills are spaced 5 feet apart, with rows at least 7 feet apart. Each hill has its own watering basin to keep fruit on dry ground.

Harvest time for summer squashes is usually 50 to 65 days after planting; winter squashes ripen 60 to 110 days later. Flood-irrigate them deeply and avoid overhead watering to foil mildew.

All the squashes grow best in fertile loams. The soil can be either sandy or clayey loam, but it must drain well. The optimal pH range is from 5.5 to 6.8.

Pests attracted to the squash family include aphids, cucumber beetles, mites, nematodes, squash bugs (its primary nemesis, especially in higher elevations), and squash vine borers. Mildew is the most common disease of the squash family.

TOMATOES. Okay. Tomatoes are a complicated subject, an almost perfect proof that gardening is an art. They are also indispensable in cookery, expensive in stores, and thus inevitable in kitchen gardens.

To get rid of a perennial question early, tomatoes are fruits that have been classified as vegetables for decades, ever since the deed was done to evade a tax.

However they are classified, when tomatoes aren't almost impossible to grow they're ridiculously easy. It doesn't seem to matter whether you understand why you succeed or fail. Veteran or beginner, some years you plant seeds and just stand back when the crop starts to come in. Some years you get terrific greenery and sparse or misshapen fruit. Some years nothing goes right.

One reason tomatoes are complicated is that they are almost perfect vehicles for breeding. If the call goes out for a square tomato, botanists can produce one at will. The size of a marble? No more trouble than the

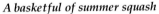

A basketful of summer squash

size of a softball. Yellow? Sure. Thick-hided? Easy. As a result, popular choice is always shifting to new varieties, many with unexpected kinks lurking somewhere in their gene pool. Beyond that they seem to be unusually sensitive to the variation between growing seasons. To cite but one example, when a warm-season tomato variety runs into a string of unusually cold nights during blossom time or just after its fruit has set, it may stop growing and never get going again.

The length of the ripening period is an important consideration for all varieties. Growers in cool areas should seek out early ripeners. Gardeners in warmer climates have a much broader choice: they can indulge in several varieties or stagger several plantings of the same variety to extend the season. The typical gestation period from seedling to ripe fruit is 50 days for early varieties, 90 for the latest ones.

When shopping for tomatoes, one question to ask is whether the variety is determinate or indeterminate. Determinate varieties stop growing at

a bushy 3 to 5 feet tall and produce their full crop in a relatively short period. Indeterminate varieties grow steadily until autumnal frosts kill them. Some get up to 14 feet high. They produce crops over a long season . . . and usually need it, because they are slow ripeners compared to their determinate kin. 'Big Boy' is one of the best known of the indeterminates.

Other climatic-factor demands must be met once tomatoes' lust for warmth has been appeased. Beefsteak varieties, for example, need not just heat but humid heat; they do ex-tremely well in the South and Midwest but not so well in the dry Southwest. Because of the scores of variables to consider, local inquiry is the best guide to selecting a really satisfactory variety.

All tomatoes fare best in highly organic soils, especially sandy loams. Clay soils should be heavily amended with organic matter before planting. Their preferred pH range is from 5.5 to 6.8.

A fertile soil at planting should eliminate the need to fertilize during

the growing season; tomatoes are not vigorous feeders. In fact, heavy nitrogen feeding produces bales of foliage and not much fruit.

Tomatoes can be started from seed or as nursery-bought seedlings. Gardeners who start from seed usually keep the plants in a green-house or indoors until they are a couple of inches tall before trans-planting them. Part of the reason is to protect them from frost—another part is to thwart earwigs, snails, and slugs, which will all feed on tender young shoots.

At planting, space seedlings 2 to 4 feet apart in all directions, depending on the variety. Tomatoes will root deeply, so they can get by with less frequent watering than many other vegetables. But they still respond well to a deep mulch to help keep soil temperatures as steady as possible. Seedlings need water every other day. A deep soak every 10 days is about right for mature plants.

Seedlings may need protection from spring frosts; hot caps or similar covers work well. Bushes should be supported by wire cages, stakes, or trellises. Do not use thick metal supports; they get hot enough to burn the stalks.

Tomato hornworms are persistent pests but can be controlled easily by diligent hand picking. The principal enemies of tomatoes are verticillium wilt, fusarium wilt, and nematodes; the preventative is to keep moving tomatoes from site to site within the garden. Once soil is infected, your only recourse is to plant resistant varieties, which are labeled by resistance. The familiar three are V, F, and N for verticillium, fusarium, and nematodes. A variety may be resistant to any one, two, or all three. More recently, breed resistances have been identified on labels as FF (race 1 and race 2 fusarium), T (tobacco mosaic virus), A (alternaria leaf spot), and L (septoria leaf spot).

Tomatoes also are somewhat sus-ceptible to mildews and molds. Blossom end rot is a mystery malady, best controlled by a consistent water-ing program that does not let soil dry out. Sometimes adding calcium to the soil will help control this rot.

'Celebrity' tomatoes supported with stakes

FRUITS

APPLES. At least 7,000 known varieties of apple exist today, a staggering number from which to choose. And because apple trees will live for 60 years, making a satisfying first choice is crucial. The first key factor is how much cold the variety can stand without freezing and how much chill it must have for the kind of dormancy that leads to full crops of flavorful fruit. Most apple varieties are so attuned to specific climates that it is hard to grow good fruit in regions that do not suit them. The second key factor is disease resistance, which goes hand in glove with climate. The third key is how the fruit will be used: for dessert (eating), cooking (baking or sauce), or cider. Selection should be based on all three considerations. Apples take from 2 to 8 years to bear, depending on the variety—and most varieties need pollenizers.

Most apple varieties come full-sized (to 20 feet tall with a spread of 40 feet), fully dwarfed (to 6 feet tall), or at any of several stages in between. An espaliered dwarf is often the only choice for cramped suburban gardens. Dwarfs are always easier to deal with when it comes to pest control, but you can afford to loose 10–15 apples from a full-sized tree to every 1 from a dwarf. (Dwarfs yield 3 bushels a tree, full-sized ones 18 to 20.)

Apples prosper in deep, fertile loam with a pH of 6.5, but are tolerant of a wide range of soil types and a pH of as low as 5.5. They must have good drainage; clay pan is the poorest kind of soil for apples.

Apples are modest nitrogen feeders and need preblossom fertilizing (1:1:1) only when tip growth is less than 6 to 8 inches a year.

They're prey to codling moths, apple maggots, tent caterpillars, aphids, spider mites, scab (especially where there is summer rainfall), fireblight (mainly when overfertilized with nitrogen), and—where soil is heavy and wet—several root rots. A few extreme examples: 'Priscilla' resists scab; 'Criterion' is susceptible. 'Granny Smith' and 'Idared' are mildew prone. 'Lodi' is prone to fireblight. 'Liberty' resists both mildew and fireblight.

BLACKBERRIES & RASPBER-RIES. Blackberries and raspberries are botanical cousins, greatly alike in growth habits and not all that different in flavor. In fact, blackberries differ as much in flavor among themselves as they do from raspberries. Some blackberries are so distinctive that they go by separate names—boysenberry, loganberry, marionberry, ollalieberry.

All brambles prosper in deep, rich, well-drained soil and full sun. However, depth and drainage are more important than soil texture. Because of their susceptibility to verticillium wilt, brambles should not be planted where potatoes, tomatoes, eggplants, or peppers have grown in the previous 2 years or within 500 feet of older brambles; check with your county Agricultural Extension agent for resistant varieties. The best edible plants to grow to rehabilitate soils having wilt are beans, cauliflower, peas, and summer squash.

In addition to verticillium, root rots affect brambles (none endures standing water during the dormant season), as does anthracnose. Pests include aphids, cane borers (control by pruning out infested canes when pinhead-sized holes first appear at or near ground level), mites (use a dormant spray containing lime sulfur), and strawberry root weevils.

To give new roots room to develop, work soil to a depth of 9 inches or more. Many veteran gardeners dig animal manure into new beds.

In hard-winter areas, brambles are best planted on slight slopes with good air flow. A northern exposure helps keep plants dormant until spring freezes are past. Wherever any bramble approaches its hardiness limits, the bed should have a thick enough mulch for the first-year canes to be buried in it as protection against freezing.

BLUEBERRIES. Blueberries tip their hands when it comes to growing conditions. All of them grow wild very near water—ponds or swamps for highbush, streams for rabbiteyes.

Highbush blueberries, common in the northern states, thrive in frequently watered, well-drained, acidic soil rich in organic matter—the kind that suits the rhododendrons and azaleas to which the berry is related. Bushes survive in soils with a pH of 3.4 to 6.5; they prosper in the range of 4.5 to 5.0.

Rabbiteye blueberries, the southern cousin, have similar requirements: highly organic soil with a pH of between 4.5 and 5.2 and good drainage.

If the pH is high, dig in peat moss just before planting or fertilize with sulfur 6 months before planting (contact with raw sulfur will kill the roots). In regions of high pH, plant blueberries in prepared beds of pure peat moss.

Blueberries are blessedly free of diseases and insect pests—almost their only problem is powdery mildew. Birds can be kept from ripening fruit with netting.

CHERRIES. Cherries are difficult to recommend for an organic home garden, because they are prone to many pests and diseases that do not respond readily to natural controls.

Cherries have not grown well on dwarfing rootstock that can be espaliered, ordinarily the most effective way to keep size and thus maintenance manageable.

For those who wish to persist in the face of odds, checking with a county Agricultural Extension agent for varieties that resist cracking is wise—and especially important where summer rains are common.

The trees grow best in deep, well-drained loams having a pH in the range of 5.5 to 6.5 (preferably 6.0 to 6.5). Reliable drainage is more important than fertile soil. They should not be planted in lawns, which have incompatible water and fertilizer needs.

The long list of diseases to which cherries are prone includes bacterial gummosis, brown rot, cherry leaf spot, and leaf curl. Cracked fruit after a rain is not the result of a disease, but it does open the door to brown rot. The list of pests includes aphids, bud moths, curculios, fruit moths, Japanese beetles, mites, pear slugs, and scales. Gardeners in the Pacific Northwest must add the cherry fruit fly (or apple maggot).

None of these difficulties poses so much of a threat to the crop as do feeding birds. Nurseries sell loose-woven netting to thwart them, but espaliers and dwarfs are far easier to cover than are standard trees.

FIGS. Many people erroneously believe figs to be desert plants. In fact, some varieties ripen well in cool, damp climates such as Seattle's. They can even be grown in the Midwest, providing they are severely pruned and clad in a winter overcoat of plastic film over burlap or—better—fiberglass insulation plus deep mulch around the roots. The key, even in hot-summer climates, is the proper choice of variety. (A serious nuisance in this regard is the tendency for single varieties to go by different names in different regions.)

Figs tolerate a wide range of soils. They are one of the few fruits that do well in mildly saline or alkaline ground. (Too high a pH is betrayed by tip dieback.) Rich soils produce too much foliage and not enough fruit; so does excessive fertilizing with nitrogen. Figs do not need fertilizer until tip growth is less than 1 foot per year.

Figs—especially their above-ground parts—are troubled by few pests or diseases. The roots may be attacked by nematodes, and in California pocket gophers pose an even greater threat to roots. The solution is to plant the figs inside chicken wire "baskets" large enough to contain a healthy root system.

GRAPES. Grapes are at once enormously versatile and uncommonly particular. The versatility comes from having thousands of varieties within three main families. The particularity comes from breeding the varieties to prosper only within a very narrow climate range.

Vitis vinifera is by far the most versatile species. It is the great wine grape, the only raisin grape, and the favored table grape. Within the *vinifera* species, the 'Muscat' group holds most promise for home gardens. The vines bear heavily, and the grapes are outstanding for eating fresh when grown in a wide range of climates. Other table and raisin grapes—'Perlette', 'Thompson Seedless', 'Tokay'—are not hardy and require unusually high temperatures to ripen. Unless you live where these grapes are grown commercially, they are poor prospects. Similarly, the great wine varieties—'Cabernet Sauvignon', 'Chardonnay', 'Pinot Noir', 'Riesling'—are so highly attuned to climate that they cannot be expected to do well where wineries have not already shown the way. In any event they are not much good for eating or making jellies (they lack pectins) or for any use other than wine making.

Vitis labrusca is North America's native grape species. Strongly flavored, winter hardy, and needing no unusual heat to ripen, it grows all across the northern tier of the United States. 'Concord' is the most famous varietal name and is even more famous as a flavoring (in grape jelly, grape popsicles, grape juice), but there are many other red and white members of the *labrusca* species. 'Concord' and its kin are also sought for eating fresh; they make strongly flavored wines.

Vitis rotundifolia is more commonly known as the Muscadine. Needing humid heat, it is limited to its native range, the southeastern United States. Botanists debate whether it is truly a grape or just something similar. *Rotundifolias* stand apart from other grapes by the need of some varieties to be pollinated. The grapes are best used in jams and jellies—they are less than excellent for eating fresh, and make wines that are even stronger in flavor than the Concords.

All species of grapes perform best in sandy or gravelly loams that drain well, though a few varieties of each tolerate heavier soils; the optimum

pH range is from 5.5 to 6.5.

Grapes do not often require fertilizing, though some gardeners boost crops of table grapes by applying a balanced fertilizer just after spring growth begins.

Both principal pests of *vinifera* grapes attack the roots: phylloxera (a root louse) and nematodes are best controlled by resistant rootstock. Check with your county Agricultural Extension agent to find out which rootstocks perform well in your area. Leafhoppers are sometimes a problem, but sulfur inhibits them. In the Pacific Northwest, grape mealybug can be controlled with dormant oils. Netting protects against depredations by birds. Mildews and molds are the major grape diseases; sulfur dust or Bordeaux mixture are the usual controls.

PEACHES & NECTARINES. Several traits other than the fuzziness of the peach and the waxy smoothness of the nectarine separate these two fruits, but both are peaches to the eye of a botanist. Certainly they can be treated identically by gardeners.

Among the many varieties, some are adapted to almost every American climate; a few newer ones even tolerate the humidity of the coastal lowlands in the southeastern United States. That climate harbors too many rots to let the fruit of older varieties ripen and has too little winter chill to drive the trees into the full dormancy they need.

Peaches thrive in sandy loams and pure loams, but can perform in heavier soil if they have good drainage. For best results the pH should range between 6.0 and 6.5, though the trees will get along in pHs as low as 5.5.

These are heavy nitrogen feeders and may also need occasional feedings of zinc, boron, magnesium, and potassium. The usual sign of zinc deficiency in peaches is small leaves clustered at the tips of otherwise bare branches. Most gardeners apply an all-purpose fertilizer each spring at budbreak to avoid all problems.

Both peaches and nectarines are somewhat disease prone. The list includes brown rot, canker, various

Peaches ready for picking

leaf spots, mildew, peach leaf curl, and scab. Brown rot and peach leaf curl are the most troublesome— 'Belle' is particularly susceptible to brown rot, which can be controlled by dormant sprays containing copper or lime sulfur.

Principal pests are borers and curculios. Aphids, mites, and scales will also pay court to peaches. Borers (the larvae of several moths) attack down to 3 inches below the soil line— wilting during the heat of the day is one symptom. A surer one is a gummy, sawdusty mass at the base of the tree. To do away with borers, scrape away 3 inches of soil. Ram wires into any holes to kill existing borers. Do not extend horizontal damage when doing so; this exposes tissue the borers left undamaged. If a hole must be enlarged, do so vertically so as not to damage any more cambium. Next, paint the trunk with tree seal. Finally, replace the soil you dug away with fine gravel. If you are planting a new tree, put a gravel collar around the base to thwart borers before they can attack. Also build a low dike to keep water from standing around the crown.

PEARS. Neither European nor Asian pears are the easiest trees for an organic gardener to grow, but the rewards are incomparable fruit.

First-time growers need to know that European pears are difficult to ripen on the tree; they are better picked green and stored in cool darkness for as long as 2 weeks to reach their juicy best. Left on the tree they tend to become hard and grainy; the same thing happens if they are picked too early. The visual cues to pick them are that one pear falls and many others show a blackened ring where the stem joins the fruiting spur. If the latter come off with only a gentle twist, pick them.

Asian pears should be tree ripened.

Although pears perform best in well-drained loams with a pH of 5.5 to 6.5, they are more tolerant of heavy, wet soils than are most other fruit trees. The European varieties need chilly winters and dry summers. Asian pears get by with less winter chill and tolerate greater summer humidity, which makes them better choices in the southeast, especially.

Pears need little nitrogen—indeed, they cannot tolerate it because of their susceptibility to fireblight. If a tree has tip growth of 12 to 18 inches a year and yields 5 bushels per standard tree, it should not be fertilized. When trees drop below these performance levels, a low-nitrogen fertilizer may be applied about every third or fourth year.

Fireblight, scab, fruit spot, and leaf spot are the principal diseases. Pear psylla, codling moths, curculios, mites, and scales are pears' primary pests.

Fireblight is the particular bugaboo of European pears. Almost overnight a branch will look as if it had been burned black without losing its shape. To forestall this, keep other susceptible plants (especially pyracantha) out of the garden, fertilize minimally, and spray with copper sulfate and lime (Bordeaux mixture) at blossom time when the temperature is 60°F or above. If fireblight appears, cut it off 6 to 8 inches below the blighted leaf nearest to the trunk and dispose of the branch far from the garden. If more than one branch is infected, sterilize the cutting tool before the first and after every subsequent cut (dip shears for 30 seconds in rubbing alcohol or a 10-percent solution of household bleach). If you are planting a pear, choose a resistant variety: 'Kieffer' is best; 'Fan Still', 'Maxine', and 'Orient' are good; 'Bartlett' is especially susceptible. 'Flemish Beauty', susceptible to scab, is not a tree for regions with summer rains.

To control pear psylla, which is more to be feared for spreading pear decline than it is for primary damage, use a dormant oil spray before budbreak and thereafter insecticidal soaps at pink bud and petal fall. The same spray program will inhibit most other insects that pears host.

PERSIMMONS. Looking for a handsome, trouble-free deciduous tree that grows tasty fruit? Looking for one that is curiously ornamental in hanging onto its globular flame-colored fruit long after the leaves have fallen? Try a persimmon.

There are two sorts, the native species and an Asian one. The native

Strawberries just shy of maturity

. . . Persimmons

tree is the hardier. Its small, tart, tannic fruit is more difficult to ripen fully—and inedible until the flesh turns mushy ripe. The Asian tree has some varieties with similarly astringent fruit, others that produce persimmons sweet enough to eat off the tree like apples while they remain as firm. Asian varieties are somewhat less hardy than peaches. All persimmons can be cooked into wonderful desserts.

The native species requires a pollenizer; several of the Asian persimmons are self-fertilizers.

The tree produces best in loamy soils, but tolerates both sandy and clayey soils. The native species takes to acidic soils better than the Asian import does, but both tolerate a fairly wide pH range. The center point is a pH of 5.8 to 6.5.

Persimmons rarely need fertilizing. If tip growth reaches about 1 foot per year and the foliage remains dark green, do not fertilize. Give them light feedings of nitrogen in spring whenever growth slows or leaves become pale.

Persimmons are so nearly pest-free that a chewed leaf is a surprise; they

are likewise rarely troubled by diseases.

PLUMS & PRUNES. In terms of fruit grown, the extended family of plums and prunes is divided into three groups: soft-fleshed, juicy Japanese plums are best eaten fresh; sweet European varieties are tops cooked or dried; and tart, tough-hided American ones are at their best in jams, sauces, and preserves. Prunes are extra-sweet varieties from Europe.

Japanese varieties require the greatest amount of heat to ripen. Another choice factor is hardiness. The natives lead in that department; European varieties are second.

Plums grow best in sandy loams with a pH of 6.0 to 6.5. Although they will grow in clayey soil, they are among those fruit trees least tolerant of poorly draining soils. Their inability to withstand wet roots also makes them poor candidates for planting in lawns.

Because they tend to set heavy crops, plums usually need annual fertilizing with an accent on nitrogen.

Insects troublesome to plums include aphids, borers, curculios,

mites, and scales. Principal diseases are bacterial canker, brown rot, and various leaf spots. The trees suffer little from these pests and diseases in warm, dry regions, though aphids, mites, and scales may necessitate an occasional dormant oil spray. Borers can be treated as for borers on peach trees. In humid climates brown rot and leaf spot will respond to weekly applications of wettable sulfur throughout the growing season. Bacterial canker has no organic cure, but can be inhibited by vigorous pruning and regular fertilizing.

STRAWBERRIES. Although the strawberries we eat are all descended from plants native to North America, years of breeding have made current varieties almost as closely adapted to specific climates as grapes are.

Choose the right variety for your location and few edible plants will reward you so well. The plants are prolific producers of one of the world's best-loved fruits. Individual plants are short-lived, having 2 to 3 productive years, but they reproduce readily. Also, they respond quickly to attention (or neglect). And finally, they can be replaced easily when they do fail.

Strawberries are fairly tolerant of soil, though they thrive best in rich, well-drained sandy loam with a pH of 5.8 to 6.5. They will not tolerate salts in soils. Soil should be tilled to a minimum depth of 8 inches to accommodate roots and assure drainage, which is vital to plants this susceptible to root rots. Raised beds are helpful where soils are heavy and wet. New plants should be set so that the base of their crown is at soil level.

Fertilizing strawberries is most decidedly an art. Some recommend feeding just as runners start. Others say the right time is just after the main crop ripens, because that helps set new buds but does not produce excessive foliage and runners. Either way, high-nitrogen fertilizers are your first choice, especially in regions with leaching summer rains. Because even with fertilizing the plants wear out in 2 to 3 years, keep young plants and grub out weary ones by cultivating.

Aphids, mites, slugs, and snails are

the primary pests—all are easiest to control by hand picking. Balk birds with netting.

Primary diseases are red stele (a root rot), yellows (a virus), and verticillium wilt. To minimize the latter do not plant strawberries where eggplant, tomatoes, peppers, potatoes, or raspberries have grown within 2 years. If either yellows or verticillium wilt does show up, move the location of the strawberry bed for at least 2 years and choose a wilt-resistant variety. Red stele is best controlled by providing excellent drainage. 'Redchief' and 'Guardian' are resistant to red stele in humid continental climates.

ORNAMENTALS

AGAPANTHUS. Sometimes called Lily of the Nile, agapanthus is an evergreen or deciduous perennial with long, straplike leaves, thick rootstocks, and fleshy roots. Thick globes of trumpet-shaped, blue or white flowers perch atop long, tubular stalks.

Agapanthus thrives in loamy soils but will tolerate heavy ones. It also needs ample water during the growing season to perform well but will survive in near-drought conditions. Because it tolerates heavy soils and is thirsty, it is much grown near ponds.

In all but very cold climates the plant is left in the ground year-round. It needs dividing every fifth or sixth year only. In cold climates it can be grown as a container plant or lifted and stored during the winter, to be replanted in spring.

Although agapanthus resists most diseases and insects, its lush, looping growth does make it a favorite daytime hiding place for snails and slugs.

ANNUALS. The long roster of garden bright spots called "annuals" includes such favorites as cosmos, dianthus (pinks), dahlias, hollyhocks, impatiens, lobelia, marigolds, nasturtiums, pansies, petunias, poppies, and zinnias.

Many of these plants are true annuals. Others are perennials but are grown as annuals.

Though they have various climate requirements and somewhat different complements of pests and diseases, most annuals can safely be lumped together when it comes to soil requirements and other matters of cultivation.

Because annuals—like most vegetables—live their lives in a single growing season, they perform best when you put them in rich, well-conditioned soil with a pH in the 6.0 to 6.8 range. As far as these plants are concerned, there is no improving the soil as you go along. Soil should be dug to the full root depth of the plants you have chosen (usually no more than 12 inches), and nutrient-rich organic matter incorporated into it. Compost, fine-ground bark, and peats are prime candidates to improve soil structure and provide at least part of the nutrients. Blood meal, bonemeal, or one of the other meals will enhance the supply of nutrients.

Annuals may be planted from seed or transplanted from flats as seedlings. Timing is critical in either case.

Seedlings transplanted into cold, wet soil will only mark time until the soil warms. The time to put them out is when permanent plants in the garden are showing new growth.

Seeds sown in cold ground will be slow to germinate. In mild-winter areas they can be put out in autumn and left to germinate on nature's schedule, or saved until early spring. In hard-winter climates, sow seeds in April or even May. Where the growing season is short, seeds can be sown in flats and kept indoors to germinate and get a head start on spring.

To sow seeds, rake the bed smooth, breaking up all clods and removing rocks. Depending on your landscaping plan, broadcast the seed or plant in rows; then cover all seeds with a layer of prepared soil or compost. Usually this layer is about twice the diameter of the seeds being sown, but check your seed packets to be sure. Soak the seedbed with a fine mist,

repeating as often as necessary to keep the surface moist. Strips of burlap over the seeded area will help conserve moisture.

Seed packets give you spacing instructions. Follow them in cooler climates; allowing plants to grow densely packed in hotter climates helps shade soil, keeping it cooler and conserving moisture.

Once the seeds germinate, protect the plants from birds, earwigs, snails, and slugs with a mesh netting at least until they have developed two sets of leaves—longer, if pest threats are substantial.

To plant seedlings from flats, prepare the soil as above for a seedbed. Water it well at least a day before you set out the plants. Try to transplant on a cloudy or foggy day. Early morning is the best time, late afternoon second-best. Late afternoon may be best for large-leafed plants like zinnias, petunias, and marigolds, because they will have the cool night hours to recover from the shock of being moved.

Soil in the flat should be moist but not saturated when the plants are to be removed for transplanting. Rather than slicing the soil, begin at a corner and try to pull each plant and the soil around its roots free from the larger mass. Set plants into generous-sized planting holes that will leave them slightly lower than they were in the flat. (An exception is stock, which should be set slightly higher.) Fill in around the root ball with prepared soil, pat it firm, and water thoroughly. Cover the bed with mulch to conserve water, inhibit weeds, and prevent soil crusting.

If you hit a hot spell soon after transplanting, shade the young plants with a screen netting of some sort.

As plants become established, water them deeply whenever the top inch of soil dries out. Overhead watering will do until blossoms begin; thereafter, flood irrigation will serve better.

For maximum bloom, apply nitrogen fertilizers at 2-week intervals for as long as the flowers last. Fish emulsion and blood meal are two prime choices of fertilizer.

Here are some notes on individual

requirements of specific annuals:

Cosmos struggles when the soil is too rich.

Dianthus (pinks, sweet William, and carnations) are more frost-hardy than many annuals but less tolerant of extreme heat. Where summers are hot and winters mild, they can be grown for autumn and winter bloom. They grow best in light, fast-draining soil and suffer when overwatered. Sweet William and carnations are subject to fusarium wilt and rust.

Impatiens require full sun in moderate climates but must have afternoon shade to blossom well where summers are hot. In fact impatiens are one of the finest hot-climate bloomers for shaded spots. They are notably useful in organic gardens because they attract people but not bugs, snails, fungi, or viral diseases. Impatiens require rich, moist soil.

Lobelia is very slow to grow from seed, so most gardeners opt for nursery-grown seedlings. The plants need moist, rich soil.

Marigolds, like impatiens, are notably resistant to pests. They may even have some value as a living pesticide: they appear to be toxic to nematodes. They are also one of the easiest of all annuals to grow from seed. A strain known as "African marigolds" requires richer soil and more water than do others. The strain called "French marigolds" contains the varieties known to discourage nematodes. Avoid overhead watering because the stems break under the weight.

Nasturtiums transplant very poorly so should be grown from seed. Curiously, the flowers are edible (they have a spicy, peppery taste) but the seeds are poisonous. They thrive in sandier soils than do most annuals and need ample sun. Aphids are strongly attracted to nasturtiums.

Pansies (and the virtually indistinguishable violas) are among the perennials grown as annuals. They are difficult to grow from seed. For fullest flower they must have rich loam and monthly fertilizing.

Petunias grow best in dry regions. Where summers are humid, look for varieties identified as Botrytis resistant. Petunias are also subject to the tobacco (or geranium) budworm; *BT* (see page 53) is the most common organic insecticide for this pest.

Poppies are easy to grow from seed but very hard to transplant. As seedlings poppies are almost irresistible to birds, so they require netting for protection. California poppies are not true poppies but rather perennials usually grown as annuals. They will grow readily from seed in the sparsest of soils, require little water, and are prey to few pests or diseases.

Zinnias are splendid growers, especially valuable where water is at a premium. Seedlings should be kept on the dry side. Grown plants should not be watered overhead; it invites mildew, sunburn, and broken stalks when water weighs down the heads.

AZALEAS. See Rhododendrons.

BULBS. From earliest spring well into summer, bulbs—crocus, cyclamen, daffodils, freesias, gladiolus, hyacinth, iris, lilies, narcissus, tulips—provide bright to outright blazing floral displays, all with little effort from the gardener.

The ideal soil for most bulbs is one that drains well but retains water for the roots . . . which is to say a sandy loam with plenty of organic content to a depth of 12 inches. Heavy clay or sandy soils both require a hefty organic amendment for bulbs to do well. In hot, dry climates, even highly organic soils should be covered with a mulch to help cool root zones during hot spells. In cold-winter areas, a winter mulch such as straw or pine needles will keep soil from repeated freezing and thawing, which damages bulbs, especially the more tender sorts such as iris.

The prevalent pests of bulbs are aphids, mites, and thrips.

When preparing a bulb bed, double digging (see page 44) is always useful to help the roots go deeper and find nutrition once they reach full depth.

If you plan to plant a large number of bulbs in one bed, it is often easier to excavate the entire bed to the proper planting depth, fertilize with bonemeal or rock potash (for phosphorus and potassium), and then position the

Camellia japonica 'Magnoliaeflora'

bulbs and cover them all at one time. The rule of thumb is to place the bulbs three times as deep as their greatest diameter; their roots will extend twice again as deep.

If you plan to combine bulbs with annuals or other perennials in the same bed, it is generally best to set out the surface plants first and then plant the bulbs. That way there is no danger of locating surface plants directly over bulbs. If you have to plant the bulbs first, mark the location of each one as you cover it with topsoil.

Soak bulbs deeply at planting; this watering should last until the tips of the leaves appear. Then water regularly after the bloom ends, until the leaves naturally turn yellow. (Do not cut off green leaves; they are a source of nutrition for bulbs that helps them store energy for the following year.) Use a spading fork, not a shovel, to dig up bulbs for replanting.

CAMELLIAS. People write whole books about camellias. Evergreen shrubs or small trees native to Asia, they already number in the thousands by species and variety. Hybridizers continue to multiply those numbers in quest of ever more dramatic flowers.

Though many varieties do well in warm-to-hot climates, they must be sheltered from strong sun and drying winds, especially when young. Plants that survive planting in full sun will prosper once they are large and dense enough for the canopy to shade their root zone, but this is doing things the hard way.

All camellias need well-drained soil rich in organic matter; the best pH balance is 5.5 to 6.5. As container plants, they will thrive in soils at least 50 percent organic. If the soil is kept fertile, camellias will do well in the shade of large trees.

Camellia trees more than 3 years old can be expected to survive on natural rainfall except in the driest regions. Where they are irrigated, you must be careful to prevent salts from accumulating in the root zone. If your irrigation water is salty, leach the accumulation every year with two deep soakings per summer.

The most common disease of camellias is petal blight; its symptom is browning of petals that quickly extends into the center of the blossom. (Browning just at the outer tips may be a result of sun- or windburn.) The cure for petal blight is proper sanitation. Pick up all fallen flowers and dispose of them in the garbage; also pick and dispose of any infected blossoms. If you have a mulch under the plant, rake it up and replace it with a fresh, deep one. (A thick mulch helps prevent fungus spores from becoming airborne.)

Most other problems of camellias are a result of uncongenial doses of sun, fertilizer, or water. Scorched or yellowed areas in the center of leaves usually mean sunburn. Burned leaf edges, excessive leaf drop, or corky spots on leaves are signs of overfertilization. Yellowed leaves betray iron chlorosis. Excessive bud drop results from over- or underwatering.

Camellias should be pruned just after flowering.

RHODODENDRONS. One of the showiest, most popular, and most populous of garden shrubs numbers more than 800 species with more than 10,000 varieties. If it's any consolation, that total includes all of the plants we call "azaleas."

Rhododendrons and azaleas differ greatly in their adaptation to climate: rhododendrons are better suited to the cool and wet, azaleas to the warm and dry. Beyond that their cultural needs are quite similar.

They need acidic soils with a pH of 5.0 to 6.0 and a large proportion of air in their root zone. They also require voluminous moisture at their roots. This seemingly contradictory requirement of plentiful moisture and fast drainage should endear rhododendrons and azaleas to organic gardeners, because it implies a high proportion of organic material in the soil. This requirement reflects, incidentally, a greater susceptibility to root rots.

This recipe for a raised bed to avoid heavy soils and poor drainage shows exactly what is needed: 50 percent organic matter (of which about half should be peat), 30 percent

soil, and 20 percent sand. Beds should be raised at least 1 foot, more often 2 feet, to keep the roots out of slow-draining soils.

A constant mulch of pine needles, oak leaves, or conifer bark helps maintain soil acidity.

Because rhododendrons and azaleas require frequent watering, they may be subject to a buildup of salts in regions where water contains dissolved salts. Where this occurs, root zones must be leached free of salts at regular intervals: irrigate with enough water to drain through the root zone three times.

These difficulties aside, rhododendrons and azaleas are little troubled by pests or diseases. The most frequent pest is a root weevil, the larvae of which feed primarily in spring. Control is difficult using organic pesticides.

One other note of caution: rhododendrons and azaleas put out feeder roots right at the surface, so soil within the root zone should never be cultivated.

ROSES. Roses are one of the great treasures—not just of the garden but of poets and painters as well. If the poets are right, these flowers come as near to perfection in form, color, and scent as humans dare to imagine. And they keep on coming through a long season—when the grower has done all the right things.

For all their glories, roses are not the easiest plants in the world to grow. Organic gardeners accept some extra handicaps when they choose to plant them.

Roses have been bred for so long to such specific ends that many species and varieties will tolerate only a narrow range of climatic or other conditions. The subject of rose cultivation is so vast and complex that it can hardly be broached in a short summary. One hint may help narrow your choice: regions with cool summers are best suited to pastel-hued roses with relatively few petals. Deep-colored types look muddy there, and those with many petals seldom open fully. Conversely, warm-summer regions do best with deep-colored, many-petaled roses. Pale ones

(Continued on page 92)

THE BASICS OF WATERING

Effective watering is one of the finer arts for a gardener to master. How often, how much, and how are the primary questions gardeners ask themselves.

How Often?

How often to water is doubtless the most vexing question of the three, because the answer depends on the weather and season as well as on the specific plant. Mature trees hardly ever need to be watered to survive, unless they have been imported from damper climates to a desert. Look around your own neighborhood at trees on abandoned properties. They may be struggling, but deep roots keep them hanging in there, year after year. Shallow-rooted perennials, on the other hand, do not last long without additional water to help them through the dry season. Common sense is your best guide—but here are some general rules.

1. Help all plants send roots as deep as they will grow, right from day one. Deep-rooted plants have a substantial cushion against drought compared to shallow-rooted ones.

This means good, long soaks with long intervals between, not skittish little sprinklings every day. Roots stay where water is; if there's only a bit of water, all in the top 2 to 4 inches, that's where the roots will grow. If it's deeper, roots will plunge after it. Then the top 4 inches can dry out in two blistering weekend days while the next 8 inches remain properly moist. (See pages 16–17 for some typical root depths of common garden plants.)

2. Watch the weather. High temperatures, low humidity, and wind cause rapid evaporation, not only from the soil but from plants themselves. (Plants have a few tricks for minimizing evaporative loss, but they are not magicians.) When the weather heads toward such a pattern, water more often than you do when days are cool and humid.

3. Heed the season. Plants need more water during the warm growing season than they do when the light begins to be low and wintry, days are short, and not much new growth is being generated.

4. Consider your soil type. Clay is structured so that water percolates through it slowly. Sand, on the other hand, lets water drain down swiftly. Loam falls in between. Plainly, a long interval between soakings won't have the same effect on all three types.

One rule works all the time: if the top 3 to 4 inches of any soil are dry, it's time to water. Another works in the heat of summer: if leaves wilt during the day and do not recover in the evening, the roots are not getting enough water to supply the plant. It's time to water.

A useful trick is to plant a shallow-rooted indicator plant at the drip line of prized permanent plants with deeper roots. When the indicator plant droops, water is getting scarce for the ones it is protecting.

How Much Water?

Judging how much to water is a good deal more straightforward than judging how often. The size and age of the plant and the type of soil provide most of the clues you'll need. Big plants take a lot of water; small ones do not. Nothing could be simpler.

As for soils, not only do clays and sands give up water at different rates, they take in different amounts in the first place. All soils have what is called a "field capacity," which is the maximum amount of water the soil can hold against the pull of gravity. Clay not only clings to the water it absorbs but also retains the most; sand does not retain the comparatively small amount it absorbs for very long. Again, loamy soils fall between the extremes.

Here are two fairly common watering situations. They should provide a starting point from which you can decide how much you'll need to water during the growing season to encourage deep roots.

For a tree with a 25-square-foot root basin (the area under its own drip line), a hose that delivers 2 to 3 gallons per minute, and a watering basin about 6 inches deep:

■ In clay soils, fill the basin and let it drain four times consecutively; allow it to drain completely each time.

■ In loam, fill the basin twice, allowing it to drain completely between fillings.

■ In sand, fill the basin once. If it drains so swiftly that you can't fill the basin, increase the flow to 5 to 10 gallons per minute and let it run for 10 to 15 minutes.

These guidelines will get water down to roots 6 feet deep.

For a 4- by 5-foot flower bed:

■ In clay soils, sprinkle for a total of 50 minutes, stopping occasionally if runoff begins.

■ In loam, sprinkle the bed evenly for 20 minutes.

■ In sandy soils, sprinkle for 10 minutes, being careful to water the bed evenly.

Connecting flexible tubing for drip irrigation

These guidelines will get water down to roots 2 feet deep.

How to Water?

There are three basic watering methods: sprinkling (artificial rain), flood irrigation (just what it sounds like), and drip irrigation (a highly selective diversion of water to each plant's root zone by means of low-pressure tubing). Each method has advantages and drawbacks.

Sprinkling. Overhead sprinkling is the simplest way to apply water evenly over a large surface. Many plants that thrive in cool, rainy climates respond best to this kind of watering. Many other plants benefit by having the dust washed from their leaves occasionally. Sprinkling also helps discourage some pests, particularly spider mites.

The drawbacks are that sprinkling wastes water: wind carries some of it away; it evaporates in hot, dry weather; some lands on concrete walkways or other spots where it does no good. In regions with warm, humid summers, sprinkling can be counted on to encourage black spot, rust, and other foliage diseases. Plants with weak stems or heavy flowers may also break under the weight of water applied from above.

Flood irrigation. This is the method of choice for getting large amounts of water to the deep roots of large shrubs and trees. It also works well with vegetables planted in rows. Another plus is that it minimizes the splashing of soilborne fungi or bacteria onto the lower leaves of plants susceptible to such diseases.

For flooding to work with trees, you must form a basin by mounding earth several inches high around the drip line. (The trunk must also be protected from water remaining in contact with it.) For flooding vegetable rows, furrows should be shallow and wide rather than deep and narrow. Furrows should also be in place before the roots form extensively, to avoid damaging them.

Drip irrigation. Hoses or flexible tubes with perforations or emitters save water by distributing it directly to the root zone of individual plants. In regions where drought is frequent and water supplies short, it is far and away the most efficient method of irrigating. And it shares flood irrigation's advantage of keeping water off the leaves of plants susceptible to molds and related diseases.

Scores of commercial systems are available that work with different water pressures and emit water in different ways. The lone drawback of a drip system is that it tends to allow salts to build up in the soil in regions where water has a salt content.

Climbing rose 'Mrs. Sam McGredy'

. . . Roses

bleach paler in the sun, and those with few petals often go from bud to fully open in just a few hours.

All roses fare best in well-drained soils with a high organic content. Raised beds may be necessary where the climate is wet and soil heavy.

At planting the soil should be worked as deep as practicable, so roots can grow quickly in it. Roses need abundant potash and potassium in their root zones to flower profusely, so veteran growers take extra pains to mix rich sources of those nutrients into the soil at planting.

After planting, roses perform best when they get regular feedings. In most climates the first feeding should come just as growth begins; feeding should stop several weeks before the first hard frost.

Roses need regular watering as well as regular feeding. Because of the diseases to which roses are prone, either drip or flood irrigation serves in most regions. The exception is extremely hot, dry climates where overhead sprinkling may be required.

The primary insect pests of roses are aphids, mites, caterpillars, rose chafers, rose midges, thrips, and borers—plenty, in other words.

Rose midges are nearly microscopic. The larval form does the damage, after it hatches from eggs deposited on new tip growth. The only natural control is hand picking egg-laying adults or the larvae. See the chapter titled "Managing Pests and Diseases" for natural controls of the other insects in this list.

Because the three major diseases of roses are only slightly susceptible to organic control, rose growers more than most gardeners quickly learn to admire the wisdom behind the old saying that an ounce of prevention is worth a pound of cure.

Black spot, powdery mildew, and rust are the Big Three of rose diseases. Powdery mildew is geographically universal. Black spot and rust seldom overlap territories.

To minimize all three, plant roses in full sun and give them free air circulation. Shady sites increase disease susceptibility. (The exception is where summers are extremely hot; afternoon shade is preferable in this situation.) Crowding roses too close together or otherwise wedging them into tight spaces inhibits air circulation too much.

Once plants are properly sited, the next line of defense is consistent garden maintenance. Prune every year to get rid of disease-infected canes and keep plants open to air circulation. Keep the ground free of fallen leaves, and pick and destroy infected leaves as soon as symptoms show up.

Finally, devise a watering scheme that takes diseases into account. In all but hot, dry climates this means keeping water off the leaves except to control powdery mildew or occasionally to wash off dust.

Powdery mildew thrives when days are warm and nights are cool. Unlike black spot and rust, it spreads on dry rather than wet foliage. Although it must have moisture to survive, all it requires is humidity in the air, so foggy mornings and sunny afternoons are ideal for it. In climates where mildew is prevalent, dampen the leaves in the early morning with a fine, misting spray. This allows them to dry enough so that the other rose diseases cannot benefit from the dampness.

Black spot, the most devastating of rose diseases, is a particular problem where summer rains are common, but overhead watering may create conditions just as favorable. Wet leaves, warmth, and splashing water encourage its swift development. Drip irrigation rather than overhead watering may stop the infection and will at least slow its spread.

Rust is less likely to kill a rose than is black spot, but it's still a serious disease. Ideal conditions for it are warm days, cool nights, and wet leaves. Again, drip irrigation is least likely to encourage the spread of this disease. Flood irrigation is your next-best bet. If a plant becomes infected, pick off all its old leaves—as well as any obviously damaged ones—at pruning time.

If you must irrigate roses with a hose and nozzle, avoid as far as possible spraying the foliage and take care to keep the ground beneath the plants and other breeding spots for disease free of fallen leaves.

ORGANIC LAWNS

Most homeowners who are just turning to organic gardening think first of edible plants, only second of ornamentals, and hardly at all of lawns. But for an organic garden to succeed, grass must be included in the program, too. Otherwise chemicals used on the lawn may leach into other plantings—and at the very least the lawn clippings will be unsuitable for compost piles.

Organic or no, well-drained sandy loam is the most congenial soil type for lawn grasses. The rule of thumb for judging acceptable clays and clay loams is that standing water on bare soil should disappear within 3 hours of the end of a rain. Heavier clays should be amended with compost, manure, sawdust, or peat moss to improve drainage (watch out—compost and manure may contain weed seeds).

For a healthy lawn, the soil pH needs to be kept between 6.0 and 8.0, preferably right at 7.0. In regions where soils tend to be strongly acidic or alkaline, the pH should be tested every second year and rebalanced as needed. Your county Agricultural Extension agent can recommend effective amendments for local soil types.

A consistent fertilizing program keeps soil and turf healthy to resist diseases and pests and also helps the turf knit tightly enough to crowd out weeds. Recommendations vary widely depending on soil, climate, and species of grass. Most call for four feedings a year. The key application in most regions is 1 pound of actual nitrogen per 1,000 square feet of lawn in autumn, after the last mowing but before the ground freezes. The others are spaced about equally, or when lawn growth slows enough for periods between mowings to increase from 1 week to 2. However, local adjustments may be vital; several diseases prosper when fertilizers are applied in excess.

Manures are the most common organic fertilizer for lawns. They are most effective when the ground is warm.

Of the three lawn planting methods—seeding, sodding, and planting stolons (or plugs)—sodding is the most efficient at minimizing weeds, the quickest to become established, and by far the most expensive.

Cool-season grasses—bent, fescue, bluegrass, rye, and redtop—grow well from seed if the watering program is steady from sowing until the turf is sturdy enough to be mowed. The trade-off for lower cost is hand weeding, especially during the first 1 to 2 months.

The best strains of subtropical grasses—Bermuda, zoysia, and St. Augustine—are often seedless, so they must be planted from stolons if they're not sodded. Stolon planting also leaves the lawn vulnerable to weeds until the turf is well knit.

MAINTAINING A HEALTHY LAWN

Lawns are subject to damage from several insects, but diseases are a more frequent problem. In most cases, poor nutrition is the culprit and correct nutrition the cure.

If a lawn is still in the planning stage, it may be best to defer planting until you develop rich, biologically active soil where the grass is to go in. This is your best first defense, though a consistent fertilizing program is required over the long haul.

Two other important elements for keeping a lawn healthy are consistent watering and dethatching. The latter—removing the tangle of outworn parts of turf just above the crowns—allows air and water to penetrate to the roots and eliminates refuges of certain pests. Some rotary lawnmowers have dethatching devices, but the most effective means is to rent machines designed especially for the task. The job needs to be done every year or two.

It was once thought that bagging lawn clippings slowed the development of thatch. That is no longer the conventional wisdom. Clippings, especially if cut fine, are now viewed by many organic gardeners as self-composting sources of nutrition, best left where they fall.

The following are the most common pest and disease problems of lawns.

LAWN PESTS

Lawn billbugs. Billbugs get their name from the long snout that puts them among the subclass of beetles known as weevils. Symptoms of their half-inch-long, brown-headed, white-bodied, legless larvae at work are patches of dead grass, especially in Bermuda grass. Affected patches can be lifted up because the roots have been chewed through. Old lawns in warm inland areas are most susceptible. To control billbugs, try ryania or rotenone. Predator nematodes also may be of help.

Chinch bugs. Small, dark gray insects, chinch bugs fold their translucent wings flat on their backs when at rest. The wingless nymphs are red. Early symptoms of their feeding are patches of bleached and withered blades of grass; later, the grass dies. Chinch bugs thrive in hot weather and are particularly attracted to St. Augustine and zoysia grasses—but they sometimes feed on bluegrasses and bent grasses. Sunny spots and drought-stressed grasses are most susceptible. To verify their presence, push a bottomless can into the soil just at the edge of a withered patch; fill it with water. If chinch bugs are present, drowned ones will float to the surface. To control, water consistently. Shading lawns may also make them less susceptible to damage from this source.

Cutworms. This larval form of a number of night-flying moths is described fully on page 61. Cutworms feed on grass blades and crowns, leaving small, brown, irregular patches of damaged grass. To detect them, soak a square yard of lawn with 1 tablespoon of household detergent mixed into 1 gallon of water. This will drive the larvae to the surface. If five or more come up, treat the lawn. Routinely control by dethatching the lawn—thatch is the cutworm's daytime hiding place.

(Continued on next page)

Sod webworms. The larval form of whitish to buff-colored moths, sod webworms get their name from their habit of spinning silken tunnels in thatch layers of lawns. Patchy brown areas are your clue to their presence. Sometimes birds make pencil-sized holes in the turf while digging for the worms. To detect them, soak a square yard of lawn with the detergent mixture described for cutworms. If 15 or more worms appear, treat the lawn. Routinely control with regular watering, aeration, and dethatching.

White grubs. The larval forms of may beetles, june bugs, and Japanese beetles are identifiable in having three pairs of legs and assuming a C-shape when at rest. They are an inch or longer. Symptoms of their work are brown spots where the roots are so eaten away that the grass can be rolled back like sod. All types of grass are susceptible. Check the lawn in July: if you find more than one grub per square foot in the soil, treat it by drenching the affected area with ryania or rotenone, making sure the treated area extends at least a foot beyond visible symptoms. Predatory nematodes may become useful controls, though present experience is not yet conclusive.

LAWN DISEASES

Fairy rings. The signs are rings of dark green grass, sometimes dead zones inside the ring, and (in spring and autumn) tan mushrooms up to 2 inches in diameter at the perimeter of the ring. Fairy rings thrive in mild, moist weather. To correct, aerate the soil mechanically, soak the rings daily with water for 1 month, and fertilize.

Fusarium patch. Symptoms are browning and thinning of turf in erratically shaped spots up to 8 inches across. Cool, wet weather promotes the disease, which favors bent grasses but is possible on most species. To correct, improve air and soil drainage and avoid giving excessive nitrogen. Spreading 2 pounds of sulfur per 1,000 square feet each year may also be useful.

Helminthosporiums. These are a related group of stem and crown rots detectable by yellowing and thinning turf or by tan to purple spots on blades. Moist conditions encourage development. They're most common on bluegrasses and rye grasses. To correct, water only in the morning, remove thatch regularly so grass does not become matted, and avoid excessive nitrogen feeding.

Leaf rust/stem rust. Symptoms are yellowing of leaves and yellow to red-brown powdery growths on leaves. Rust grows under many conditions, most commonly on bluegrasses but also on perennial ryes. Increase nitrogen fertilizer, water infrequently but deeply during dry periods, and mow often. Include a resistant grass in the mix when reseeding.

Red thread. Symptoms are bleached or tan-colored areas up to 2 feet across with wiry-looking red strands (the visible part of the fungus itself) growing in the affected area. It plagues bent grasses, bluegrasses, fescues, and rye grasses. Cool, moist conditions favor its growth. To correct, apply a high-nitrogen fertilizer, especially in autumn. Minimizing shade on the lawn may also help control this disease.

Snow mold. There are at least two forms. Gray snow mold causes irregular dead, bleached areas up to 2 feet across, with gray mold visible on the leaves. Pink snow mold produces light brown circular patches, sometimes with pink fungus. Affected grass pulls up easily. Both forms prosper in wet cold, especially when snow cover lasts for long periods. To correct, avoid late-season, heavy fertilization; aerate and improve drainage; try to reduce snow pileup.

Take-all patch. Symptoms are thinning or dying out of turf in circles up to 3 feet in diameter, followed by an invasion of weeds. High moisture favors its development, but symptoms do not appear until the grass is under moisture stress. Take-all patch is most often found in bentgrass lawns. To correct, use a balanced fertilizer in autumn, avoiding those with high lime content. Adding 2 pounds of sulfur per 1,000 square feet each year may help.

Velvety organic lawn

INDEX